How to Be Successful in Your First Year of Teaching Elementary School:

Everything You Need to Know That They Don't Teach You in School

By Tena Green

HOW TO BE SUCCESSFUL IN YOUR FIRST YEAR OF TEACHING
ELEMENTARY SCHOOL: EVERYTHING YOU NEED TO KNOW THAT THEY
DON'T TEACH YOU IN SCHOOL

Copyright © 2010 Atlantic Publishing Group, Inc.
1405 SW 6th Avenue • Ocala, Florida 34471 • Phone 800-814-1132 • Fax 352-622-1875
Web site: www.atlantic-pub.com • E-mail: sales@atlantic-pub.com
SAN Number: 268-1250

Library of Congress Cataloging-in-Publication Data

Green, Tena.
  How to be successful in your first year of teaching elementary school : everything you need
to know that they don't teach you in school / by Tena Green.
     p. cm.
  Includes bibliographical references and index.
  ISBN-13: 978-1-60138-337-2 (alk. paper)
  ISBN-10: 1-60138-337-1 (alk. paper)
  1. First year teachers--United States. 2. Elementary school teachers--Training of--United
States. 3. Classroom management--United States. I. Title.
  LB2844.1.N4G75 2010
  372.11--dc22
                          2010002103

Printed in the United States

PROJECT MANAGER: Amy Moczynski • amoczynski@atlantic-pub.com
PEER REVIEWER: Marilee Griffin • mgriffin@atlantic-pub.com
ASSISTANT EDITOR: Angela Pham • apham@atlantic-pub.com
INTERIOR DESIGN: Holly Marie Gibbs • hgibbs@atlantic-pub.com
INTERIOR LAYOUT: Samantha Martin • smartin@atlantic-pub.com
FRONT & BACK COVER DESIGN: Jackie Miller • millerjackiej@gmail.com

Printed on Recycled Paper

We recently lost our beloved pet "Bear," who was not only our best and dearest friend but also the "Vice President of Sunshine" here at Atlantic Publishing. He did not receive a salary but worked tirelessly 24 hours a day to please his parents. Bear was a rescue dog that turned around and showered myself, my wife, Sherri, his grand- parents Jean, Bob, and Nancy, and every person and animal he met (maybe not rabbits) with friendship and love. He made a lot of people smile every day.

We wanted you to know that a portion of the profits of this book will be donated to The Humane Society of the United States. *–Douglas & Sherri Brown*

The human-animal bond is as old as human history. We cherish our animal companions for their unconditional affection and acceptance. We feel a thrill when we glimpse wild creatures in their natural habitat or in our own backyard.

Unfortunately, the human-animal bond has at times been weakened. Humans have exploited some animal species to the point of extinction.

The Humane Society of the United States makes a difference in the lives of animals here at home and worldwide. The HSUS is dedicated to creating a world where our relationship with animals is guided by compassion. We seek a truly humane society in which animals are respected for their intrinsic value, and where the human-animal bond is strong.

Want to help animals? We have plenty of suggestions. Adopt a pet from a local shelter, join The Humane Society and be a part of our work to help companion animals and wildlife. You will be funding our educational, legislative, investigative and outreach projects in the U.S. and across the globe.

Or perhaps you'd like to make a memorial donation in honor of a pet, friend or relative? You can through our Kindred Spirits program. And if you'd like to contribute in a more structured way, our Planned Giving Office has suggestions about estate planning, annuities, and even gifts of stock that avoid capital gains taxes.

Maybe you have land that you would like to preserve as a lasting habitat for wildlife. Our Wildlife Land Trust can help you. Perhaps the land you want to share is a backyard— that's enough. Our Urban Wildlife Sanctuary Program will show you how to create a habitat for your wild neighbors.

So you see, it's easy to help animals. And The HSUS is here to help.

2100 L Street NW • Washington, DC 20037 • 202-452-1100
www.hsus.org

Dedication

This book is dedicated to all the teachers who make a difference, to my family, and to my editor, Amy Moczynski. Thank you for making me do my homework.

Trademark Statement

Table of Contents

CHAPTER 3: UNDERSTAND YOUR SURROUNDINGS   65

PART 2: BEING A PREPARED TEACHER   107

CHAPTER 4: YOUR NEW ROLE   109

CHAPTER 5: PREPARE FOR THE DEMANDS OF THE JOB   135

CHAPTER 8: MORE THAN AN EDUCATOR: BEING WHAT YOUR STUDENTS NEED   197

CHAPTER 9: WORKING WITH PARENTS AND STUDENTS WITH BEHAVIOR PROBLEMS   209

PART 4: TAKING CARE OF YOU   245

CHAPTER 10: PREVENTING
TEACHER BURNOUT   247

CHAPTER 11: ENDING THE
FIRST YEAR SUCCESSFULLY   255

CONCLUSION   267

APPENDIX: SAMPLE LESSON PLANS   269

RESOURCES   287

BIBLIOGRAPHY   293

AUTHOR BIOGRAPHY   307

INDEX   309

Foreword

When I was first asked to reflect and share the experiences of my first year of teaching, my mind — surprisingly — went blank. That first year had gone by so quickly that I had to sit back and think about what had just happened. As I did, the smiles and the laughter at the events that occurred and the hilarious things the students would say came back to me. It was not until after my first year was over that I felt confident knowing that despite all the things that went wrong that year and all the days I had sat in my classroom feeling completely inadequate about being responsible for 20 growing minds, I had successfully completed my first year teaching. This feeling was incredible, and I have truly enjoyed remembering both the good and the not-so-good experiences of my first year.

I always knew that I wanted to teach. As I sat in my first class of the Early Childhood Education program at the University of Central Florida with 40-something other ambitious teachers-to-be, my professor asked us why we wanted to become teachers. As we went around the room, the stories were strangely similar. They all began with, "As a child, I would pretend I was a teacher, and my friends/siblings would be my students." I wondered how many times this instructor had heard the same answer, and yet she continued to seem pleased with everyone's response. This experience made me think about how powerful this career is and the amount of passion so many people share. I tried to think back to my grade-school years, and I did not remember my teachers having this type of enthusiasm. This led me to begin questioning: What happens to the passion for teaching? Is the money really that bad? Are kids that terrible that it kills what you have dreamed about doing since childhood? Do principals and other superiors really make you do such an abundance of senseless work that it makes you feel that the reward of teaching a child is no longer worth it? As I began to complete my volunteer hours through my first semester, these questions continued to marinate in my head. I began to see the old, boring teaching styles we talked about in class when referring to what we should not do, and I could not help but wonder if I would also fall into this pattern. It was not until my senior year, which is when I met my first internship teacher, that I found my answers and hope. My instructor had been teaching for more than 40 years, and I swore her enthusiasm rivaled that of a first-year teacher. It was then that I knew I could also enjoy my job for years to come, regardless of how bad it could get.

Currently I am a second-year teacher to 23 amazing third-grade students in an incredible school called Sunrise Elementary in Palm Bay, Florida. During my first year, I did not get hired until mid-September, and school had already been in session for several weeks. Although my career was not starting out the way I had planned, I was extremely grateful to have a job in the field that I love. I was given a bare room and I was ready to work my magic, but I only had a little over a week to put my visions of the perfect classroom together. During this time period, I also had to have all of my amazing lessons strategically planned for 17 students who would be coming from five different teachers' classrooms. To say I felt overwhelmed is an understatement, but I loved every minute. My team was a lifesaver, and I was truly blessed to have had such a supportive and welcoming faculty and staff. I learned very quickly how valuable my peers were!

The advice you are going to be getting from this book is going to be like gold. Although I had incredible professors and even better internship teachers, you really do not know what you are getting into until you are neck-deep in the job and just trying to keep your head above water. I remember hearing this over and over through college and I kept thinking, "Why aren't they teaching this stuff, then?" I was paying all that money to learn about theorists and how to write five-page lesson plans instead of being taught how to manage reading groups or what to do when you have more than 20 students and no classroom support. I wish I had learned things like how to budget your money when you need supplies for your classroom center materials — a classroom library, bulletin board cutouts with a matching border, calendar activities — and what to do if you want to have a treasure box. I spent way too much money trying to have what all the other teachers had. Details like these were what I would have liked to have known before I turned the key that first day.

As you read *How to Be Successful in Your First Year of Teaching Elementary School: Everything You Need to Know That They Don't Teach You in School,* you will learn that everyone has experienced ups and downs throughout the beginning years of teaching. It definitely helps knowing you are not alone as you try to deal with the anticipation you feel as you venture out on your own into your classroom. This is when you know the training wheels are off! When you get your name on the outside of the door, you now have the ability to make your own rules, and you can make your classroom into a safe, welcoming environment for you and your students. Remember, the best resource you could ever have comes from other teachers and people who have been through what you are experiencing. What could be better than to have those resources ready for you in a positive and inspirational collection of experiences from real teachers?

This book is packed with encouragement to help guide and navigate you through your first year. This information has been compiled by those who know what you are going through — and who had wished someone would have told *them* about what to really expect.

My best wishes and hopes are that you continue to see the positive in education and remember why you got into this incredibly powerful profession. The minds of children and their futures really do outweigh the hurdles and negative aspects that come with any job. You will learn very quickly that teachers make one of the most powerful impressions on children, and it really is possible to change the life of a child. Hold this responsibility with care, and enjoy it as much as you can.

— Carol Baker, third-grade teacher,
Sunrise Elementary, Palm Bay, Florida

Introduction

Teaching elementary school is an art that requires much more than knowledge and organizational skills. One of the most important qualities a teacher must possess is the ability to connect with his or her students. If you do not enjoy children, most likely you will not be able to connect with them. Connecting with your students means caring about them as individuals and taking the time to understand each of them. This gives you the ability to give them the best education possible. This requires effort and commitment on your part, and it is a gift many teachers possess.

Even still, you are probably experiencing a common worry: Even though you like children, what if they do not connect with you? Your next thought may be, "Even if I can connect with only half of my students, the other half could throw the whole classroom into disorder."

Relax. Remember your answer as to what made you decide to take a job as a teacher — you enjoy children, and you love helping them learn. These are qualities most young people can sense in adults. The students who cannot pick up that caring vibe right away will pick it up from the other students. As for the few who are left and are terrified or suffering from separation anxiety, they will also learn to trust you if you have a positive attitude toward your students and your work. Due to your appreciation for your students, their individual characteristics, and your enjoyment of sharing knowledge, you possess the ability to connect with your students.

Now you may be wondering if that is all you need to be successful: to connect with your students. The answer to that question is no. It does take more than connecting with your students, and that is why this book is here for you. This book will ensure you have the tools you need to be a successful and effective elementary teacher throughout your first year of teaching.

It is important all teachers (temporary or alternative certified teachers, new teachers, and veteran teachers) understand they are one of the most valuable assets to our country, even to the world. Everything in our society is now global, with people coming and going from one nation to another and taking what they learn with them. Due to our society being so mobile and our nation being so diverse, the responsibilities and the value of our teachers is immeasurable, and that fact will be discussed thoroughly in the pages of this book.

Your career choice is honorable, but it is wise to be absolutely sure this is the career you truly want. The good you can do is great and will inadvertently affect many people — not only the students and their families, but every life those students touch throughout their future. Being on the brink of becoming a new teacher, you must understand that if you are making the wrong career choice, the damage you may cause could carry long-term consequences. If you mistreat a student, the child could carry feelings of mistrust for adults throughout his or her lifetime. That is why this book will take a look at your career choice and show you the qualities of a good teacher to ensure you are embarking on a journey you will enjoy.

This book is meant to be an invaluable resource for new teachers, but even more importantly, it gives down-to-earth advice that sometimes gets lost in the usual university chit-chat, where those around you may be using terms you may not yet be familiar with. Here you will find answers to questions and worries that repeatedly whisper in your mind; worries about whether your students will listen to you, or concerns of connecting with your students to give them a better education. This is a book to help you understand the exciting yet challenging journey on which you are about to embark. There will be discussions on how to be a good teacher, the students' perspective of what makes a good teacher, how your primary grade students think, and what challenges await you. This book will show you how to be prepared for that first day of school so you can earn your students' trust and ease their — and your own — discomfort upon starting something new and unfamiliar.

This book will share ideas on developing lesson plans, staying on course with paperwork, and finding the time for much-needed down time. This book's focus is to help you succeed in your first year of teaching elementary school, which will help ensure your students succeed. *In Appendix A in the back of this book, you will find sample lesson plans and activities you can implement in your classroom.*

In these pages, you will be provided with knowledge from first-year and veteran teachers, giving you the answers you need to make sure your first year of teaching is not only successful but enjoyable. You can find unique answers from experienced teachers on how to be an effective leader who will have a long-lasting influence on the outcome of what will be, over the course of a career, thousands of children.

You will see how each classroom contains diversity that can be used for the good of your students. Gifted students as well as students with special needs have much to offer, enabling you to become more effective as a teacher and make your job challenging but never boring. With this book, you will learn ways to bring a comfortable and enjoyable environment for learning. This book will help you show your students how to work together and achieve success. With the knowledge you receive in *How to be Successful in Your First Year of Teaching Elementary School,* you will have a step up on how to be a successful and effective teacher for your students, giving you more time to focus on the enjoyable side of the job.

As you read this book, you will gain knowledge of how to connect with your students, the most valuable of all tools for any effective teacher. This book will remind you as you walk into that educational facility on the first day of school, it is not only you who will be feeling anxious and excited; your students feel the same, as will their parents.

How to be Successful in Your First Year of Teaching Elementary School is a book that can be used by all new teachers today and tomorrow, providing the inspiration and encouragement needed to begin a valuable and worthy profession.

Part One:

The Job

"I decided I wanted to be a teacher shortly before starting my freshman year of college. I had already registered in the medical records field and said to myself, 'Hey, wait a minute! I love children, and I don't think I would be happy sitting at a desk all day looking at papers.' I had spent that summer teaching Bible school and Sunday school, and decided I had better change my major. Thank goodness I did."

— Malia Jarvis, kindergarten teacher at Shumaker Elementary in Bellevue, Ohio

Chapter 1

The Importance of Your Career

According to a World Bank report UNICEF posted, every extra year of primary education increases a person's productivity by 10 to 30 percent. And according to a study by Durham University's Curriculum, Evaluation, and Management Centre, the early years of education are the most crucial. This study also says the first year in a student's educational life has an effect on the final year of the student's primary schooling. Professor Peter Tymms, director of Durham's CEM Centre and author of the report, said attention should be given to every year of education, but "early-years education is critical." The emphasis placed on the early years of education makes teaching elementary age students an important job.

There are good parents and bad parents, and the same is true for teachers. Just as good parenting skills, or the lack thereof, have long-term consequences on children, so do teaching skills. According to a report on the long-term consequences of teacher placement and bad teaching written by authors Jessica Levin, Jennifer Mulhern, and Joan Schunk, bad teaching will lead a child to believe teachers are not to be trusted, and it can even lead to long-term effects, leaving the child to believe all adults cannot be trusted. Bad teaching can cause a student to give up academically, which can also cause the student to be viewed as a failure. Jobs and temporary job service employees tell their clients it is almost impossible to get a job without college credentials, and it is even harder to gain employment without a high school diploma.

When parents become upset over their child's having a teacher who treats students unfairly or screams when things are frustrating, confrontations can sometimes escalate into a situation that cannot be calmed. If a teacher and the parents cannot find a solution, the administration must step in. When the administration believes there has been physical harm done to a student, the teachers' union becomes involved. Accusations that the union protects bad teachers have been made throughout the years, and it has become so commonplace that it has caused some teachers to take a serious look at that possibility. The accusations have been so consistent over the years that there are numerous Web sites that have been created solely for the subject. A good example of this is **www.teachersunionexposed.com**. It is not uncommon for bad teachers to simply be moved to a different school because the administration feels it is easier than fighting the union to fire the teacher.

Due to these poorly qualified teachers, there have been studies on the long-term effects of bad teaching by organizations such as the National Association for the Education of Young Children (NAEYC), the Faculty of Education and Social Work at the University of Sydney, and the Rand Corporation, a nonprofit organization that did a study and produced the "Assessment of Reach and Sustainability." The New Teacher Project has done numerous studies to show there are long-term consequences when you pair unprepared or bad teachers with students; the project has stated, "Principals are often blamed for failing to initiate dismissal proceedings, but even when they try to formally terminate a teacher, the data show they face a very limited likelihood of success."

The importance of protecting teachers is critical, but after bad teaching was discovered to have long-term consequences on students, it is now obvious that provisions that were constructed to protect teachers can do a disservice to many. Some rules in place to protect our teachers "overshadow what should be the most basic aim of our school systems: the education of our children," according to a publication posted on The New Teacher Project Web site, **www.tntp.org**.

Your career as a teacher can ultimately affect thousands of children. The main concern is whether your influence will be positive or negative, which is why the decision to become a primary school teacher is an important one for many people.

Some of our most effective teachers are coming from the Alternative Teacher Certification programs. Alternative certification is a program that trains people who already have at least a bachelor's degree, along with numerous life experiences, and helps them become teachers. These programs are tailor-made and job-specific to place teachers where they wish to be and where they will be the most effective. In 1983, there were only eight states that had an alternative route to teaching, but 20 years later, there were 43 states as well as the District of Columbia that offered some type of alternative route for certifying teachers. The number of candidates who wish to become teachers is growing. The prospective teachers work with mentors while teaching and usually go through the program working with other veteran teachers. This better prepares them for the profession, giving them more skills and thus providing students with a more effective teacher.

Let us take a look at what it takes to be a good teacher in order to help you be sure of the career choice for your future.

Characteristics of a Successful Teacher

Palms sweating, heart thumping, you enter the building where you have managed to land a job as the brand-new teacher of elementary-age students. You have spent years preparing for this day, and yet you are terrified of what awaits you. A bit uncertain of what to expect, you realize your certification justifies your new position, but it does not necessarily mean you are ready. The only thing that can prepare you for your first year as an elementary teacher is gathering as much knowledge on what to expect as possible. That is why this book was written.

What if the students you are now responsible for do not relate to you? What if they will not listen? What if little Johnny's mother dislikes you and tries to make your life miserable? These questions and more run through your mind as you enter a world that seems to be total chaos. Voices of all ages echo up and down the hallway. Small, medium, and large people wander, entering and exiting doorways, rushing in the hallway where you now stand. You freeze on the spot, all your doubts and fears surfacing to the forefront of your brain and paralyzing you.

Now is when you need to breathe. Put one foot in front of the other and remind yourself that you are one of thousands who have lived and survived moments just like this one. You are going to love this job, enjoy your students, and quickly become a good and effective teacher. You are here to mold your students into young people who can become assets to their communities.

Now that you are standing in that hallway and forcing yourself to put one foot in front of the other, ask yourself why you decided to become a teacher of primary students. If your immediate answer is not because you love children and helping them learn, you may want to consider switching careers. If you are now making your way through that educational facility because you are sincere about helping children learn, then more than half the battle of becoming an effective teacher has already been won. Rest assured you are well on your way to being a good teacher.

There are teachers who have outstanding lesson plans and instructors whose knowledge puts them close to genius, but these teachers may fail at being an effective leader. So what makes a good teacher if not one who has excellent lesson plans or vast amounts of knowledge to share with their students?

Don Shinton is a veteran teacher who recently attended a meeting for cooperating teachers. At this meeting, teachers were asked to come up with the qualities they hoped to see in the teachers who were about to start working at their school. The answers epitomized the characteristics of effective teachers.

CASE STUDY: TIPS FROM VETERAN TEACHERS

Don Shinton
Fourth-grade teacher
Cheston Elementary School
Easton, Pennsylvania

"There were five groups of teachers working to come up with a list of qualities we hoped to see in student teachers we were about to get. The order of importance changed by group, but each group mentioned the same qualities:

1. **Organized:** I never realized just how organized you have to be to lead a classroom. I worked for 20 years in corporate America before I started teaching. Each night before I left my office, I would set up

my desk for the next day. It took me about five minutes, and I was ready to go for the next day. As a teacher, you are not just organizing your day, but you are organizing the day for the children you teach, so you must spend a great deal of time preparing for your day. There are always road blocks that you encounter each day, but having a strong plan for your day helps to minimize any potential behavior problems.

2. **Hard-working/Flexible:** In elementary classrooms, you have a large array of abilities. To make sure you are meeting your students' needs, you have to develop lessons that challenge them at their instructional level. This means you must spend a lot of time developing lessons that address their needs. It gets easier to do this as you build on your experience, but you can expect to work hard to make sure that your students are challenged appropriately.

3. **Dedicated:** You should expect that the day doesn't end when the last child leaves. You must show interest in your students. You will need to attend PTA meetings, after-school tutoring, and extracurricular events.

4. **Dynamic:** You want to create lessons that are challenging and dynamic. It is not about what you do; it is about what you get the children to do. You must be a dynamic leader so your children want to be engaged in the lessons that you have developed for them.

According to the System for Adult Basic Education Support (SABES), there are special qualities that make a good teacher. Maria Hassett, Ph.D., and Richard M. Reis, Ph.D., of Stanford University believe the following list contains the ingredients the best teachers possess:

- A love for children

- Enthusiasm for teaching

- Comfort with not knowing everything

- Perception of teaching as parenting

- A good sense of humor

- Constant reflection of your work

- A positive attitude

- The ability to adapt and change

- The desire to give your students confidence

- The desire to motivate your students

- The ability to listen to your students

- No fear of taking risks

- Tolerance of uncertainty

- Expectations of success for your students

- A sense of purpose

- The ability to learn from a variety of role models

- The desire to avoid stagnation in your lesson plans and class-room activities

Do not be concerned if you do not have all these qualities right away; you will learn many as you go. In addition, these characteristics are not all-encompassing; effective teachers may not possess all of these qualities, but most effective teachers do possess at least a portion of these traits in order to connect with their students and help them obtain the drive they need for success.

Effects of Good and Bad Teaching

It is widely known that children will not learn well if they receive lessons from an ill-equipped teacher. Studies show that when a student falls behind, they will continue on a path to failure if an effective teacher does not step in the following year. However, there can be factors influencing how a child develops other than just a bad teacher. Some of those factors are: their health, home environment, supportive parents and family, class size, and the quality of teachers he or she will have in the primary years of education. The student's environment influences his or her ability to be successful academically. If a student has a bad attitude and a teacher does nothing to change that attitude, that student will fail. On the other hand, if an effective teacher reaches out to help that student, giving him or her more attention, praise, and encouragement, that student has a better chance of academic success.

At one time, education was assessed in terms of enrollment and completion rates. Today, we understand this is not sufficient in assessing success, and this concept of achievement has changed. A closer look at whether children are learning and retaining what they are taught has become more important. Learning and retaining has not only educational implications, but also economic. If a student is academically successful, that student has a better chance to be socially successful.

Henry Adams, an American journalist, academic, and historian, once said, "A teacher affects eternity; he can never tell where his influence stops." Ask any successful adult if they can remember a teacher who made an impact on his or her life. You will hear stories of good, effective teachers every time.

David Diaz, a physical education teacher at Southern Lehigh Intermediate School in Bethlehem, Pennsylvania, is a good example of that fact. Diaz is a teacher today because of a teacher's influence on his life when he was a young boy. He said the reason he decided to become a teacher was because he has a great experience with his physical education teacher in middle school and high school, "and I knew then that was what I always wanted to do." Diaz also admits that to be an effective teacher you must have "flexibility, be even-tempered, specific in giving directions, and willing to make a fool of yourself." Diaz knows that a sense of humor is crucial when dealing with children; he sees about 600 students in his classes every three days.

A non-caring teacher can cause a student who is uncertain in his or her attitude about school to decide he or she dislikes school. On the other hand, a loving and caring teacher can help a student strive for success. The power you have as a primary school teacher is amazing; that power can also be scary. As long as you believe in your students and care about their future, you will be an effective teacher with a career full of rewarding feedback and respect.

Now that you know the exceptional possibilities that await you as a primary school teacher and are up to the challenge of helping students succeed, the next consideration is where you might want to teach.

Chapter 2
Where You Want to Work

Where you wish to start your career includes many choices, and to make a good choice, you will need to look at each of them in depth. To begin, let us examine these schools so you can have a better perspective on where you might want to teach.

Where to Look For a Teaching Job

There are many factors you need to consider before choosing an environment to work in. Here are some points to consider:

- Do you want to work where you live currently, or are you flexible?

- Do you currently have a specific school in mind?

- How far are you willing to travel to go to work each day?

- Is income a predominant deciding factor?

- Do you prefer having your pay spread out over the course of 12 months, or just the months that you are in school?

- What do you need in terms of benefits?

- Do you prefer an urban, suburban, or rural setting?

- Do you prefer to teach to a small group or a larger class?

- Would you prefer teaching in a public school, a private school, or another alternative, such as a charter school?

- How important is working in an environment with endless resources and the most current technological advances?

- Would you be open to the idea of teach solely online courses?

This chapter will cover four different types of schools: online, public, private, and charter schools. Of these four schools, there are pros and cons to each.

Online Schooling

Internet schooling seems to be the wave of the future. The Florida Virtual School (FLVS) is an example of online schooling; it is an Internet school that is teacher-driven. FLVS, which was founded in 1997, was the first statewide Internet-based public high school. FLVS serves Internet-based students in grades K-12. Not only does this program provide virtual education, but it is also an established leader in developing solutions for students in Florida, the United States, and the world.

Students all over the world can take courses through FLVS, but Florida residents have the right to choose FLVS as an educational option and take courses for free. In FLVS, students receive assignments and turn them in through the Internet. Students have a teacher for each course, and those teachers stay in close contact with the students through e-mail, online chats, phone calls, and discussion boards. Teachers and students have the flexibility of working from home during the hours that work best for them.

Online schooling has been around for approximately a decade, so it is still a new concept in the world of education. Due to the constant changes in technology, online learning is consistently and rapidly evolving. New programs that are more user-friendly are being made for online schooling. Watching a teacher on a computer used to be a choppy audio challenge, but better technology has made online learning as easy as watching television. With online learning, people become better educated. The more education a person has usually means a better-paying job will follow, and this gives a higher tax base for the states. Regardless of the fact that online education is a permanent education option, there are still flaws in the system. There are outstanding programs, and there are failing programs, but this is true in all kinds of schooling.

Out of 40 online schools in the United States that the Peak Group studied in 2002, there was a combined enrollment of 85,500 students. The Peak Group, which provides market research and consulting services focused on educational technology, found that at the time of the study (2001-2002), there were fewer than 1,000 online teachers in the country. It was estimated that the number of online students would reach 500,000 by 2004. In the fall term of 2005, it was reported that there were nearly 3.2 million students taking at least one online course. These students range from elementary-level students to adults taking college classes.

With online schooling, you can be a full-time instructor or teach a single student for extra income. While most instructor positions are for colleges and universities, each year there are more opportunities for elementary, middle, and high school distance-learning teachers. Salaries for online teachers can vary anywhere from $12,000 to $50,000 a year, depending on the number of students you have, bonuses, and accreditations.

FLVS was awarded the Excellence in Distance Learning Programming, Pre-K – 12 Education Award from the U.S. Distance Learning Association in 2003. Since that time, FLVS has won numerous awards, at least one per year, and the latest was in 2009: the Software and Industry Association's CODiE Award for Best Virtual School.

This program offers a wide range of courses from science to writing. Students are assigned a teacher who works with his or her students in a hands-on approach, speaking with one another on the phone, through e-mails, and via chat boards. Students and teachers work together every step of the way, and parental involvement is strong.

In FLVS online schooling, teachers are expected to make phone calls to speak with the student and their parents at least once a month. Teachers also create monthly progress reports. In this line of work, you are available to your student at all times, through e-mail and by phone, making it convenient for students and parents if they have questions. The parental involvement sets FLVS apart from all the other online schools because it plays a major role in making the school a success.

Online schoolteachers work hard in making individualized learning programs, suggesting classes and lessons that are particular for that individual student. But as with any type of job, online schooling is not for every teacher. There are many benefits to being a teacher for online schooling, including no tardy students, bullies, absences, class disruptions, morning commutes, or after-school rush hour traffic to deal with. Another positive aspect in online school teaching is you will get to know your student more thoroughly than you would in a classroom. You will provide one-on-one learning and will speak to your student one-on-one on a regular basis.

Some suggestions for being successful as an online teacher include:

- Organize a separate space in your home and use it solely for your workspace.

- Make separate increments of time for different duties such as dealing with administrative paperwork, responding to message boards or e-mails, and grading.

- Make sure your students have a syllabus and ensure that your policies for due dates or research are understood by the student and the parents.

- Make your calendar as detailed as possible, including dates for tests and papers due.

- File your e-mails for each student.

- Create templates for welcome e-mails, test and report reminders, and office hour notices. Include an emergency number as well, because students should be able to contact you any time, within reason.

- Be patient with yourself and your students. First-time online students and teachers can feel overwhelmed, especially if they are learning new programs when they start.

A disadvantage to online school teaching is that because you are working at home, you may have a hard time drawing the line between work life and home life. This is true with any work done from home, and if the line is not drawn and boundaries are not made, it can cause misunderstandings with family and your social life. Also, online teaching requires a large amount of time, especially when you consider that you are on-call to answer any questions a student may have. Again, boundaries must be set, such as setting specific times when you are available to take calls.

Traditional Schooling

Traditional schooling has three options explored in this section:

- Suburban schools
- Rural schools
- Inner-city schools

Although brick-and-mortar schools in America are in no way going to be replaced by online schools, there are many considerations a beginning teacher should look at before jumping at the first job that becomes available.

It would be neglectful if overcrowding were not brought to your attention, especially when considering suburban and inner-city schools. Overcrowding is a nationwide epidemic because school districts do not have the money to keep building schools to keep up with the growing student population. A shortage of qualified teachers adds to that problem and creates a major dilemma with long-term consequences.

Let us look at suburban schools first, as they usually have more to offer in curriculum and necessities for teachers than other forms of public schools.

Suburban schools

Some of the pros to working in a suburban school include:

- Average to above-average income areas result in greater taxes and increased funds

- Increased funding provides for better supplies, materials, and field trips

- Better overall resources that are less likely to be outdated

- Lower dropout rate

- Greater overall achievement rate, which some studies suggest is directly proportionate to the income levels of the surrounding area

- Increased security to combat challenges

- A wider range of courses available to students

Many of these schools have a better base of income than many rural or inner-city schools. Suburban schools are located in areas that have average-income families, which allows the school district to offer better wages that can attract teachers who would otherwise prefer to work elsewhere.

Most suburban schools are located in areas surrounding a large city, and for the suburban school districts, homeowners abound. Thanks to homeowners and jobs located within the school district, there is a good tax base that is derived from the homeowners' property taxes, giving suburban schools more money. The tax money used for schools is mostly obtained through property taxes, but there are also taxes paid by businesses that go to the local schools. According to statistics found on the Bureau of Labor Statistics Web site (**http://stats.bls.gov/oco/ocos069.htm**), the average salary for kindergarten, elementary, middle, and secondary schoolteachers in suburban schools ranged from $43,580 to $48,690 in May 2006. Earnings of $28,590 to $33,070 were the lowest 10 percent of annual earnings.

Studies show that the students in suburban areas are more likely to come from average-income families. At one time, only 10 percent of suburban students in the United States qualified for free lunches, compared to 40 percent in the inner-city schools and 22 percent of those who live in rural areas. Under the 2008-2009 federal guidelines, the cut-off income line for a family of four to receive free lunch was $27,560.

While there are significant advantages to working in a suburban school setting, there are still some cons to working in one of these schools. Some cons to working in this environment include:

- Increased family income may cause entitlement and apathy among students

- Potential for decreased cultural diversity, depending on area

- Not a significantly challenging teaching environment

- More desirable neighborhoods create greater competition for jobs

- Larger pool of applicants may lead to lower salaries and decreased benefits

Rural schools

Just like suburban schools, rural schools offer several advantages and disadvantages. Some of the pros to working in a rural school include:

- Generally smaller class size

- Less competition for jobs

- Slower pace for those who prefer this lifestyle

- Potentially safer environment

- Supplemental income and resources from programs such as Rural Education Achievement Program

One program that has been advantageous for rural schools is the Rural Education Achievement Program (REAP). Some rural districts lack resources, and REAP is supplemental income for these schools. When a school receives grant allocations that fall short in helping them attain their goals, REAP steps in and gives additional monetary support. These system changes are already taking place and showing promise for improvements in the rural school districts. An example of this is Lyme Elementary School, which is located in Bellevue, Ohio, a rural area inhabited by mostly farmers. At one time, Lyme School did not have connection to city water lines and was forced to have water hauled in. While this was common for the area, it was expensive for the school district. Years later, thanks to REAP, Lyme Elementary no longer had to have their water hauled and was connected to water lines that ran from a nearby city.

There are several disadvantages to working in a rural school you should consider before applying for a teaching position at one of these locations. These cons include:

- Limited district funds translate into decreased curriculum offerings

- Potential for decreased cultural diversity, depending on area

- Poverty is an issue

- Not a significantly challenging environment

- Distance between locations is generally farther, equating to a potentially farther commute

- Potentially outdated resources and materials

- Less technology for educational purposes

- Decreased program options

- Higher dropout rates at the high school level when individuals begin working to take over the family business

- Confusion and despair in areas where farmland is sold and developed

- Lower self-esteem and lower achievement rates among students

- Lower salaries

- Fewer jobs

- Increased responsibilities for teachers

Poverty plays a major role in rural schools due to the lack of jobs in the areas. Most of these schools depend on state and national funds, so if the economy is not doing well, rural schools are not doing well, either. Most rural schools are isolated, geographically and culturally. Due to the isolation, it is harder to get materials needed for teachers and students, and it also requires a major effort to network with people. Farms are disappearing because farmers are selling their farms when they cannot make ends meet, thus schools are preparing students for a different way of life, a different society, and a change in tradition. Once, students of farmers would grow up and take over the family business; now, they must prepare for a different way of life.

Rural schools are normally small schools, so they get less money from the government because the government gives funding based on the number of students enrolled and the students' needs. Many of the school buildings are in need of repairs, making the learning environment less than motivating and sometimes unsafe. It is also common to find these schools do not offer Advanced Placement and honors classes. Most of the materials you will find in rural schools are outdated, and technology is often not available or extremely limited. The textbooks these schools use are often old due to the schools' lack of funding. There is also limited access to technology in these areas because of a lack of towers and fiber optic lines for computers and phones, but this has been improving over the years.

It has been shown that rural students have lower self-esteem and a higher dropout rate. According to a report from the National Center for Educational Statistics (NCES), urban dropout rates are about 50 percent higher than rural rates, but there has been a discrepancy in how the statistics have been gathered over the years. NCES also points out that, "In some rural school districts, the dropout rates are between three and four times the national average rate." In July 2008, California State Superintendent of Public Instruction Jack O'Connell said, "…we had to rely on complicated formulas (before the new Statewide Student Identifier) to make educated guesses about how many students were graduating and how many were leaving with a diploma." Due to rural areas' being isolated, jobs are less plentiful, and the population tends to be that of mostly aging adults. Because there is a shortage of jobs in the area, there are no new residents moving into the community. The decrease of homeowners and workers in a community means the need for state and federal government funding increases because of a lack of taxes for the schools to pull from.

Another major problem with rural schools is the shortage of quality teachers. In rural areas, teachers face many challenges: low salaries, lack of professional opportunities, and multiple duties, such as recess monitor or lunchroom monitor. Rural schools receive fewer applicants and have a high teacher turnover rate. These teachers' experiences, salaries, and locations are secondary compared to those of suburban and inner-city schools. Without quality materials, rural schools will continue to have a hard time educating their students.

Inner-city schools

Inner-city schools are a host for complex issues for many teachers. Some of the problems teachers in inner-city schools face are:

- Lack of funding stemming from impoverished areas

- Outdated textbooks and a lack of resources, creating problems with the curriculum

- Overcrowded classrooms and potentially rundown facilities

- Students with significant problems outside of school

- High student turnover and an increased dropout rate

- Apathetic students creating an overall lower achievement level

- Potential for insecurity, fear, fatigue, and stress are greater for new teachers, particularly if they are unfamiliar with the environment

Teachers in these schools are challenged more than most, especially new teachers. With the cultural differences due to more minorities' being located in cities as well as stretched resources, it does not take long for beginning teachers to become overwhelmed. Even though there is diversity in the teaching staff, the cultural differences in students — and the added work due to these cultural differences — can be overwhelming for teachers.

The turnover rate in urban schools is astronomical. According to the National Center for Education Statistics, (**http://nces.ed.gov/programs/coe/2008/section4/indicator31.asp**), five years seems to be the average amount of time a teacher will last here if he or she is not prepared by a mentor. To make matters worse, these teachers do not just quit; they totally give up on the profession.

Many teachers do not want to work for inner-city schools because of the diversity; the problems students bring to the classroom from living in poverty; and the funds for supplies being so low. Also, the extreme diversity of students means many needs that teachers will have to cater to, such as cultural differences and students who speak broken or no English. There are students with health issues due to poverty-stricken families' having no medical insurance, emotional problems from broken homes, and students who are left on their own because the parents have to work more hours to get by financially.

Children living in urban areas are more likely to be living in poverty. Inner-city school students are sometimes known as "project students" in reference to their homes — living in the housing projects. According to the 2008 Online Encyclopedia, some 9.7 million children between the ages of 5 and 17 speak a primary language other than English at home. Of those, about 1.3 million children do not speak English well or at all.

Children who live in urban areas tend to change schools more than other children. According to many school principals, today people are more mobile, and it is not uncommon for some students to attend three or four different schools in one school year. There are schools in the United States that report their student enrollment changes daily, such as Brevard County schools in Florida. High student mobility does affect a child's education, and the child is more likely to be behind grade levels in reading and math. Most of these students will repeat a grade.

There is a strong reluctance among certified teachers to work in urban schools; therefore, Alternative Certification programs have been implemented. These certification programs offer less demanding time constraints for training and attract older, more diverse individuals who have more life experiences. These programs are offered at a lower cost and provide more teacher support in mentoring. Such programs are available in many states, Texas and Missouri being two. The need for mentoring rises in states such as Texas because of the number of students who speak limited English. The individuals who take part in these programs believe they can make a difference for inner-city students, and they go into the program fully aware of what they might face.

It has become common knowledge that something must be done to help new teachers who decide to teach in urban schools. A program called Learning to Teach in Inner-City Schools (LTICS) was created to help eliminate some of the disparities in teacher preparation and was based on individual student and environmental differences. This program helps new teachers understand the cultures and communities of inner-city students, and shows teachers how to use positive behavior modifications skills. LTICS also helps new teachers learn how to manage classrooms in inner-city schools, giving them tips and skills that are unique for these educational institutions. How to teach students who cannot speak English is one example of what these teachers learn.

To combat the problem of the teacher dropout rate in urban schools, another program for inner-city schoolteachers came to fruition in Birmingham, Alabama. This program is known as the Urban Teacher Enhancement Program (UTEP), which was designed by the University of Alabama at Birmingham's School of Education. UTEP is a degree program that recruits teachers from a variety of backgrounds and is funded by a federal partnership grant, Training and Retaining Urban Student Teachers, which was designed to increase the number of teachers who can survive the tough, urban academic environments. The training in UTEP emphasizes social competence, diversity issues, affirmed attitudes, and students with special needs.

While there are drawbacks to teaching in an inner-city school, there are also positives. Some of the pros to being an inner-city teacher include:

- Potentially higher salaries.

- Signing bonuses to attract new teachers.

- Cultural diversity.

- Potential offers from schools to pay off your student loans.

- A strong need for good teachers in these areas.

- A challenge and an increased sense of accomplishment when success is achieved.

- Assistance available from programs, such as the Center for Urban School Partnerships at Texas A&M University (**http://tlac.tamu.edu**). The CUSP center researches and offers support to projects on collaborative learning in urban education environments. One of these CUSP initiatives offers mentoring for veteran teachers through professional development for urban teaching.

Urban districts are more likely to use salary incentives to attract teachers, giving them a one-time sign-on bonus, especially for those who take jobs in undesirable locations. Urban districts also use salary incentives when there are unfilled vacancies, showing there are salary fluctuations in districts that have trouble hiring teachers. However, please be advised that urban elementary and secondary teachers earn about equal salaries as that of other types of schools. Teaching high school is when the higher pay rate comes into play, but the one-time sign-on bonus is usually offered to all new teachers.

As a teacher in an inner-city elementary school, you will be forced to be more creative in finding resources and new ideas to be successful in your career. Also, if you are someone who likes to be challenged, inner-city schools may be the place for you, as you may find more satisfaction in your daily routine. More importantly, your successes with your students will be major successes, and if you are going to be a teacher who thrives on helping your students, this is a great place to work. In inner-city schools, you will find that teachers gain immense satisfaction upon knowing they have helped students overcome hurdles.

Private schools

Most educators decide to work in a private school regardless of decreased pay. Teaching in a private school will sometimes pay $10,000 to $15,000 less than public schools due to lack of state and federal funding. Regardless of the decreased pay, there are many teachers who prefer working in a private school because they feel these institutions have a friendlier environment. Although some private schools now offer pay that is close to that of public schools, the reasons teachers decide to work in private institutions are usually based on other factors, such as smaller class sizes and stricter rules for students.

Most private schools are religious schools. In the school year 2007-2008, there were 33,740 private schools in the United States. That number includes secular, non-secular, and charter schools. At that time, 78 percent were religious institutions. The U.S. Department of Education estimated that 49.8 million students attended public elementary and secondary schools in 2009, and more than 5 million students attended private schools.

There are two major options that allow families to use state funds to send their children to private schools — tax credits and school vouchers. In the tax credit system, families pay for their child's tuition using their own money. These families are given tax credits when they file their state income taxes. Under the voucher system, families are given a portion of the student's school tuition that comes from the state. In 2002, the U.S. Supreme Court allowed for voucher programs that are religiously neutral but provide secular school options.

Some factors to consider when looking at private schools are students, curriculum, certifications, class size, and pay. In considering students, private schools can be, and in most cases are, selective about whom they admit into their schools. Because the cost of tuition is so expensive, most of the students come from homes that are more financially secure. There are also limited funds from both the state and federal government because of laws separating religion and state. This leaves less funding available for hiring specialized teachers, so you are less likely to have special-needs students in a private institution.

In a private school, the government has less control over curriculum and state requirements, and the state-mandated tests are optional. Some private schools will use their own tests to determine the students' progress rather than the state-mandated tests; many teachers feel this is less of a burden for them to carry. Rather than having to focus on preparing the students for state-mandated tests, schoolteachers can focus on teaching lessons and perhaps prepare their students for a test enforced by the school in which they are working.

In private schools, you may not be required to have certifications or explicit degrees to teach your subject area, which is another reason someone might consider teaching in these educational facilities. In public schools, it is not uncommon for a teacher to specialize in English but be forced to teach math; this rarely happens in private schools.

One of the main selling points of private schools is class size. According to a report by the National Center for Education Statistics, for the 2009-2010 school year, the average class size in private schools was estimated to be at an average of 13 students per teacher. It is also easier for private schools to remove disruptive students from the enrollment list due to greater parental involvement. In private schools, parents are well-informed of rules and regulations, and generally agree with them.

Even though you will have more control over curriculum in a private school, you must also realize that many times you will be expected to include religious material in your daily teachings. Some teachers may not have a problem with this requirement, but there are those who prefer to keep education and religion separate; therefore, this aspect should be thoughtfully considered.

Though having more control over curriculum and smaller classes is beneficial, the lower pay scale is usually the determining factor for most teachers. However, another big advantage to working in private schools is the minimal bureaucracy involved, as the administrative side of the job is much less time consuming. The administrators for private schools do not have to abide by some state standards, leaving more time to support their teachers and their students. This is also better for the teachers because it gives them more freedom to teach lessons without worrying about state standards.

Charter schools

Charter schools are the center of a growing movement that challenges the traditional methods of public education. Since state legislatures began passing charter legislation in the 1990s, more than 4,000 new schools have been established. Charter schools are causing states to create something entirely new in education by allowing these schools to be exempt from selected state or local rules and regulations. In 2006-2007, these schools were serving more than 1.2 million students. According to the Center for Education Reform, there were a total of 4,578 charter schools serving more than 1.4 million students in the United States in 2008.

Charter schools run independently of the public school system and tailor their programs toward the community's needs. These schools are looked at as a way to increase educational choice by educators, parents, and poli-cymakers. According to the U.S. Charter Schools Web site (**www.uschar-terschools.org**), these educational institutions are operating with freedom from many of the requirements that apply to traditional public schools, such as state-mandated testing. Charter schools are chartered to establish a "performance contract detailing the school's mission, program, goals, students served, methods of assessment, and ways to measure success."

People establish charter schools for various reasons, and the founders are normally parents, teachers, and community members. The three reasons most cited for starting charter schools are educational vision, independence, and serving of special purpose. Teachers, community members, and parents feel that by starting their own schools, they can give the students in their community an educational vision that serves their needs for that particular community. They also feel that by being independent, they can focus on what is more important for the students in their facility, rather than having the state dictate what is educationally important. By serving just their students, they are fulfilling a special role instead of serving the purpose of students scattered over hundreds of miles.

Charter schools serve an average of 250 students, meaning smaller class sizes, and parents associate safety with smaller schools; this is one reason parents choose to send their children to charter schools. Another reason parents choose charter schools is because of their higher academic standards. Many times, the educational philosophies charter schools offer are in line with their own, which is another reason why parents choose these institutions over public schools.

The benefits of charter schools include:

- Increased opportunities for learning

- Access to quality education for all enrolled students

- A system of accountability for teachers

- Encouragement of inventive teaching

- New professional opportunities for teachers by periodical assessment and training

- Parent and community involvement

- Improved public education for their particular students

In charter schools, the teachers and students are accountable for academic results, rather than held accountable for compliance with rules and regulations. Charter schools are public schools of choice; students and teachers have the freedom to choose a charter school. They do not have most of the regulations that apply to traditional public schools, and usually offer teachers and students the authority to make their own decisions as to what should be taught, when to teach it, and how to teach it. Each state varies in laws applying to charter schools because individual charters have a unique mission and goal, and because the laws significantly influence the development of these schools.

According to the Center for American Progress, the pay for teachers in charter schools varies. Performance-based pay is given more weight in the overall compensation package than it is in traditional public schools. With enough experience and credentials, pay can start at $31,500 for teachers, but normally starts around $26,000 a year. This can increase to more than $63,000 per year, depending on the contract between teacher and school, and the incentive pay for student achievement. Most charter schools evaluate teachers in different areas to determine their pay.

Now that you have more information on various schools on which to base your decision, it is time to prepare for the interview.

The Interview

You are ready to look for a job, but sometimes it is overwhelming to know where to begin. Are you ready to be interviewed? Do you know what you will say when you are bombarded with questions? Do you have any idea what to expect? Will you be interviewed by one person or four? Do you have a list of questions to ask at the interview? Let us take a look at how you can prepare yourself.

If you do not have portfolio to use when applying for teaching jobs, it is time to make one to prepare for applying and interviewing for jobs. Your portfolio should contain a résumé, teaching certificates, recent observation reports concerning your student teacher work (if you went to school to become a teacher), a copy of degree(s) earned, samples of lesson plans, letters of thanks or recommendation, and any professional development certificates you may have. When looking for a job, check for job fairs in big cities and at universities.

The following are some tips and advice for your job search. Keep in mind every state is different, so some of these tips may not apply:

- **Decide what type of school you want to teach in.** The next step is deciding which school district you would like to work in. If you do not know the districts in your area, go to the public library and look in the *Patterson's American Education* book for a list of every school district for every state. For a small fee, you can also find information on public and private schools in every district in the country through the American School Directory Web site (ASD) at **www.asd.com**. The information found here is gathered directly from each school that is listed. This information covers public, private, and Catholic schools, and grades K-12. If you want free and more in-depth information on the area as well as the school, you can discover everything from the number of schools in a city or small town in a particular state, to the amount of pollution it has. This information can be found on City–Data.com, at **www.city-data.com**. Once you have decided on a school district, you can call the board of education and request an application. Most school districts offer the applications online so you can print it at home, fill it out, and mail it in without having to call and ask for the application.

- **When you have the application, make a practice copy.** By making a practice copy, you will not feel pressured and worried about mistakes. When you have your practice copy filled out the way you want it, you can fill out the original. Be sure you have your basic biographical information, a list of schools where you have previously taught, and any other work experience you may have, because you will need this information for the application. For the list of schools where you have taught, your student teaching experience is fine if you have it; be sure to know all the information needed, such as the name of the school, the name of the district, the address and phone number, and how long you worked there.

- **Provide references.** Your most important reference is the cooperating or supervising teacher from where you had your internship or any other teaching experience. A letter of recommendation from your college supervising teacher is also a good addition if you studied education in school. If you had the principal of the school in which you worked observe your teaching, you may use him or her as a reference. Another good reference is the professor in your major area of college. For all these references, you will need their name, phone number, and address. It is not only polite, but appropriate to ask these people if you may use them as a reference before putting their name on an application.

- **Be certain of the top three preferences you list as choices for a teaching assignment.** It would be unwise to apply for a teaching position that you are uncomfortable with.

- **Consider substitute teaching until you can find a full-time position.** Being a substitute teacher is a good way to get your foot in the door and get noticed; it will also give you more teaching experience and more references. Being a substitute teacher in a district where you want to apply can be especially beneficial. If you are substituting in a district in which you would like to work, do all you can to meet the principal. If this happens, be sure to introduce yourself and give him or her some positive feedback on the students, the school, and the district.

Before you go in for an interview, there are a few things you need to prepare for:

- **List all your strengths, your experiences, and your skills.** Some people do this mentally, but others find it helpful if they actually write this information on paper.

- **Practice for the interview questions.** There are numerous Web sites that list interview questions for teaching jobs (*some sites are listed in the Appendix*). For example, the career resource center Web site of Lesley University in Cambridge (**www.lesley. edu/services/crc/interviewforteachers.html**) offers many tips for students who are looking for their first teaching job, including a list of questions you can expect during an interview.

- **Do research on the area the school district is in so you are somewhat familiar with it.** If you know and understand the requirements and the community of the job opening, you will make a good impression on the interviewer. Having this knowledge shows you have done your homework and are sincere about wanting the job.

- **Plan what you are going to wear to the interview long before time for the day arrives.** You do not want to be rushed or upset due to a hole in the shirt you were planning to wear to the interview, or because your forgot to pick up your best suit from the dry cleaners.

- **Know how to get to where the interview is going to take place.** Do not simply print directions and forget about it until the day of the interview. Days prior, go to the school or board of education and make sure your directions are accurate. Pay attention to the traffic and note if it is heavy in that area. If so, you may want to leave early.

- **Arrive early on the day of the interview.** Remember, it is never acceptable to be late, no matter how much experience you have or how good your references are.

- **Take extra copies of your résumé, your credentials, and your portfolio.** Sometimes there is more than one person sitting in on the interview, and they will each appreciate having a copy of your information.

From the moment you walk into that building until the moment you leave, you will need to be on top of your game. It is possible, and even likely, that anyone you see or speak to will be asked to give an opinion of you. Be on your best behavior, and be sure to smile.

It is possible only one person will interview you. If this is the case, it will most likely be a principal, superintendent, or human resources personnel. It is also possible that you will interview in front of a panel with as many as six people. Those people may consist of the principal, the superintendent, or members of the school board.

While it is true that most interviews follow a similar pattern, each one is unique. Regardless, you will most likely enter a room where the interview will take place. At this point, you want to shake hands with your interviewer or interviewers and start to build some rapport. Usually the first question is, "Tell me about yourself." Eventually, the interviewer(s) will bring up the position and the district. You will be asked a number of questions to determine if you are a good fit for the position. Most interviews will likely include some of the following questions:

- Why did you choose to become a teacher?

- How did your university prepare you to be a teacher?

- What do you feel are your strengths and weaknesses?

- What part of teaching appeals to you most/least?

- What is your philosophy on teaching?

- In your opinion, what is the most important part of teaching?

- How will you incorporate special needs children in your classroom?

- What does diversity mean to you?

- How will you create a positive environment in your classroom?

- How will you integrate technology into your lesson plans?

- Where do you want to be in five years?

- Why do you want to teach in this district?

- What curriculum areas do you feel are your strongest?

- What grade do you want to teach and why?

- How will you involve parents in the classroom?

- What do you know about [the grade you are applying to teach] developmentally?

- What is important in the grade you are applying to teach?

- Can you describe rules, both yours and the school's, for a classroom of the grade you are applying to teach?

- How will you create relationships with your students and their parents?

- What do you think will provide you the greatest pleasure in teaching?

- In what ways will you encourage creativity in your classroom?

- Can you describe a successful lesson?

- What do you look for in a principal?

- How would you communicate with administrators?

- What part of this job do you look forward to?

Your best response to these questions is to be honest and take your time — remember, the interviewer(s) expect you to be nervous. Each district will be different; some districts ask only a few questions, and others ask several of the questions listed and more. It is best to answer them as thoroughly as possible.

Another question to give thought to is, "What are your strengths and weaknesses?" Keep in mind that even your weaknesses should be strengths. An example of a good answer for a weakness would be, "I have a tendency to create my lesson plans for the whole year before the school year even begins." With this kind of answer, they are not going to view your tendency as a weakness. When the interviewer(s) inquire about your weaknesses, they do not expect what someone usually perceives as weak, but rather a strength that can be somewhat bothersome or annoying. They certainly do not want to hear that you sometimes lose your temper or that you have a tendency to scream when the students will not listen. These are things that could reflect badly on the school and the district, and that is not what they want to see in you as a prospective teacher.

Some interviewer(s) prefer to do a behavioral-based interview. This type of interview is based on questions about past behavior, skills, experiences, and knowledge. Some interviewers feel this information will allow them to know what your future performance might be by basing it on what your past performance was in a similar situation. Be sure to have specific examples of your skills in your portfolio, because it is the best preparation for a behavior-based interview. Some sample questions you may face are:

- Tell us of a time you had to deal with a student who was disrupting your class.

- Describe a team project you have done.

- Tell us about a difficult situation you were in, how you handled the situation, what the outcome was, what you learned from it, and what you would do differently if a similar situation occurred today.

- Describe how you would handle an angry parent who escorts her or his son into the room in the morning, angry that the student was placed in the wrong math or science group.

- Explain what you would say if a parent calls you out of concern for his or her child's low grades.

While you are being interviewed, you need to remember that you are interviewing the school as well. As much as they want to be certain that you are a good fit for them, you want to be certain this school is a good fit for you. You do not have to wait until the end of the interview to ask your questions; you will be able to tell the appropriate time to do so. If you feel you need to take an index card with your list of questions, this is acceptable. The following questions are examples of what you may want to ask your interviewer(s):

- What administrative or other tasks are required outside of teaching hours?

- What is the teacher turnover rate at this school?

- What is the average class size at this school?

- Do all teachers participate in extracurricular activities?

- Is there a set curriculum? (Remember, some private schools are not required to follow the state curriculum to the letter).

- Do you have regular staff meetings?

- Can you tell me about the students who attend this school?

- Is there a support system or mentor program for new teachers?

- Are there in-service training opportunities for the teachers?

- How active are the parents in this school?

- What is your vision for your school?

- How do your grade levels support one another?

Do not ask about pay, pensions, or sick days until you are offered the position. This is considered inappropriate and tells the interviewer(s) your priorities are not in order.

Doris Rayburn, a veteran teacher of 35 years, suggests you have questions and ask them at any interview because there are certain details you will need to know about any job you are offered.

CASE STUDY: TIPS FROM VETERAN TEACHERS

Doris Rayburn
Second-grade teacher
Mooreland Heights Elementary School
Knoxville, Tennessee

"New teachers come from varied backgrounds and training. Questions asked during an interview might be different based upon these. I would ask about school expectations for the students and system expectations for the teachers. I would ask if there is a mentoring team in place in the school, and how and when a grade level meets to collaborate on plans, units, and testing schedules. I would ask about class size, the school calendar, length of the school day, and special areas like music, art, physical education, languages, and more. I would also ask about any extra duties such as bus duty and cafeteria duty. I would ask if there is a school-wide discipline plan or if each teacher devises his or her own class discipline plan. I would ask if there are support personnel such as guidance counselors, personal accountability classes, and/or teaching assistants and time schedules for these people. I would ask any questions that I could think of that would acclimate me to the school — and remain positive when asking these questions."

It is good to ask if there are students with special needs in the school. If the answer is yes, inquire about help from special needs teachers or teacher assistants in your classroom, because having students with special needs sometimes requires extra work on your part. You will want to be prepared to work with these students and realize it will take more time, such as meetings with the family at Individual Education Plans (IEP) meetings, which take place at school. Some questions you may want to ask about special needs students and the school include:

- Will I be working alone or as a team while special needs students are in my classroom?

- What would you state is the general attitude of your school regarding special needs students?

- With inclusion, what has been the largest teacher/student ratio for your teachers thus far?

- How do you determine if the IEP is met by teachers for special needs students?

Once the interview is over, be sure to send a thank-you note. In the note, you should again express your interest in working for that particular district. Also be sure the note is addressed to your interviewer by name.

Very seldom does anyone hire in a hurry anymore, especially with a weak economy. Do not be impatient or think the worst if you do not hear from any of your interviewer(s); you will hear something in time. Keep in mind that any teachers who are already under contract must be placed before administration is allowed to start hiring new teachers. There are no set rules for when a principal or superintendent will hire. Some will hire new teachers as soon as school is out for the summer, while others will wait until the day school starts. Keep this in mind while you wait to hear from your interviewer(s) or start to feel anxious or impatient.

Now that you know a bit more of what to expect and how to prepare for the interview, you will stand out from the other interviewees. To better prepare for the job you will eventually be offered, take a close look at your surroundings.

Chapter 3

Understand Your Surroundings

When you are hired as a teacher, you are immediately part of a community. In order to better understand your new community and environment, you must first learn about your surroundings. You will be working with other professionals, and it is important for you to be able to share ideas and resources with one another. In order to get along with the staff and ensure this can happen, you need to explore the community in which you will now live.

Discover your new environment, starting with the town or city in which you will now work. Go to the local restaurants and speak with the people who are working there. Attend the local community theater, and introduce yourself to the people around you. Be present at a play or Little League game and get to know the parents. The locals will notice your presence and be curious about who you are, so this is a prime opportunity to introduce yourself to them. Getting a feel for the community will help you better establish a connection with your work colleagues, your students, and their parents.

Learn more about your students by reading their files, but keep an open mind while you are doing this. Do not pre-judge any student because of test scores or a teacher's comments regarding past behavior because a child's behavior will vary from year to year. There are also other factors that may have applied at the time of the test, such as problems at home or a death in the family. Many times a teacher will blame the student for problems when the only problem that exists is a conflict of personalities. This is a prime example of bad teaching or a closed-minded teacher who can cause negative long-term consequences.

Once you have learned some details about your new community and students, you should get the policy handbooks for your school district and school. Studying these policies takes time — something you will not have an excess amount of once school begins. District and school policies are an important source of information that you need to be familiar with.

Now it is the time to familiarize yourself with your school. Locate the offices, supply room, gymnasium, library, teacher's lounge, nurses' office, and cafeteria. You will want to know where all the restrooms are located and learn the emergency plans for your particular school, which you can find in the office. The more familiar you are with your school, the more comfortable you will be on that first day of school and all the days that follow.

Expectations of Administration

Remember, you are now an employee of a district or a board of education. You signed a contract when you took this job; therefore, you are expected to teach the district's curriculum and abide by their rules and regulations. Their policies are now your policies whether you agree with them or not, and your administration's goals and missions are now your goals and missions.

As for curriculum, it is a constantly changing product. Do not disregard or disrespect the curriculum, because a district committee and your colleagues most likely created it. It may help to think of what you have learned about your new community because local citizens pay for your district and its services.

Your administration will expect you to do your job perfectly from day one. Many times teachers are not trained on the job but are simply thrown into the classroom and told to get the job done. Your administration will also expect you to do your part in helping the district reach its goals. You will do this in several ways, including serving on committees, meeting with parents, going to meetings, and attending in-service programs and conferences. There will also be college classes and workshops that will help you reach your and the district's goals. The missions and goals stated in the front of the handbooks for your district and school are important pieces of information to familiarize yourself with.

Simply put, your administration can make your job better or make it harder than it has to be. It is important you keep your administration happy because they are the ones who will determine whether your contract will be renewed. New teachers will often get the toughest schedule, such as recess duty or cafeteria monitor, but if your administration sees you as a hard worker, they will most likely lighten your burden as soon as possible.

Your administration will consist of a principal, sometimes an assistant principal, a superintendent or manager, and a school board. The two people who will report on your work are the principal and the assistant principal; they are the administrators you need to focus on the most. They are the people you will report to, and they have the ability to make decisions on your future.

It will be up to you to find new instructions for your students. You may have to make some necessary changes in those instructions for students with special needs. This is an area your administration will pay close attention to; they will expect your efforts and modifications to be precise and effective.

Your administrators will want you to be a team player. Remember, they will be watching and waiting to see if you can keep your students under control at all times. In their eyes, you are an ambassador of your school. If your students' parents like you, that means they will like the school. If the parents and students complain about you to the administration, you will be viewed as a poor teacher, and there are some schools that see too many discipline referrals to the office as a failure in classroom management. Be sure you are always consistent and fair with the discipline you dish out in order to do your job correctly and to show your best classroom management skills. Always remember that your administrators will expect you to be professional at all times. How you act inside and outside the school will be a direct reflection on the school, the teachers, and your administration.

The expectations of your administrators are deeply ingrained in their educational values; there is nothing that will sway them from those beliefs. Your best bet is to play by their rules and play like you mean it if you wish to keep your job when it comes time to renew your contract.

According to author W. Michael Kelley, there are five types of administrators. Those five types are:

- **The Controller:** Someone who must control everything. This administrator likes to have his or her hand in everything, including your lesson plans and how you present them.

- **The Politician:** This individual is more interested in becoming the superintendent or being promoted than doing the task at hand.

- **The Nice One:** This kind of principal or manager does no managing. All the teachers know they can push him or her around.

- **The Sad-Story Buyer:** A principal who will let the students get away with almost anything if told a sad story.

- **The Ideal Boss:** A principal who feels his or her job is to oversee, and your job is to teach, so this principal hires you and gets out of your way.

Each of these types of administrators has a different personality and a different reason for their behavior and drive. It is in your best interest to figure out which of these personality types your administrator is and to adjust your teaching habits accordingly.

On a good note, your principal is the one who hired you, so obviously he or she has faith in your potential as a teacher. It is his or her job to ensure the teachers in his or her building are fulfilling their role in the educational process every day. As long as you do your job with as few waves as possible, your administrator is going to be happy with your job performance.

As an elementary teacher, you will periodically be observed by your principal or supervisor and possibly the assistant principal. Depending on where you teach, you may be observed by other people involved with the school system. Regardless of who observes you, all observations are done the same way: They sit at an empty student's desk, watching you, listening to you, observing how you interact with your students, and writing their opinions on what they see and hear. You will be extremely nervous the first few times this happens, but after that, it will get easier, and you will become less anxious.

You will never be completely free of the jitters during observations because you know these observations go into your permanent record. Your permanent record cannot be full of negativity if you are ever going to receive tenure, which is job security for teachers who have completed probation periods. The length of a probationary period varies among states but is usually three years. Just keep in mind that almost all teachers receive tenure and that a principal's job is to help you succeed.

Every meeting you have and all interaction that takes place with your principal are very important. Everything that takes place in your school falls under the jurisdiction of your principal. When you receive a request from your principal, complete the request as soon as possible; you want your principal to see you as a reliable person and a conscientious teacher.

The principal depends on you and your colleagues to make things run smoothly, as does the rest of the supervisory staff of your district. Veteran teacher Carol Baker knows how important it is to follow administration's expectations and advises you do so for very good reasons.

CASE STUDY: TIPS FROM VETERAN TEACHERS

Carol Baker
Third-grade teacher
Sunrise Elementary School
Palm Bay, Florida

"Remember to do what you should be doing at all times. It is crucial to know who your administration is and what they expect of you. Once you have this information, do it — not just some of the time, but all of the time. You never know when your administration will stop in or ask to see your lesson plans. Be prepared to defend what you do in the classroom, because you do not want them to have to continuously come to bat for you because you were not doing what is expected of you. If you are doing what you should be doing, your administration will be pleased."

With this in mind, remember that the chain of command should be followed at all times. When you do not follow that chain of command, it is seen as a lack of respect for your colleagues' positions. In many schools, especially large schools, there is usually a department head or grade-level teacher who serves as a contact between teachers and administrators. The next person in the chain of command is the assistant principal. At the top of the chain in your particular school is the principal, and at district level you will have curriculum coordinators and assistant superintendents who report to the superintendent of the schools. Above the superintendent is the school board; the members comprising this group are the supervisors of all the employees of the school district.

There are many people in charge when it comes to running a school. You may not meet all of them right away, and it is even possible that you will not meet all of them the first year. Even if you do not meet them, it would be wise to know who they are and learn what position they hold. Do not be intimidated by people who are your supervisors. Keep in mind that everyone who works for the school district is there for the same purpose.

Each community elects their district's school board. It is not uncommon for some of those board members to be parents of children enrolled in the district's schools. The school board oversees the development of curriculum and sets policy. The board also manages the district's funding and spending, as well as makes decisions for the district. It is in your best interest to get to know their names and faces. After all, it would be embarrassing to see them inside or outside the school and not recognize them. This would be especially bad if they approached you, and you found yourself totally ignorant of whom you are speaking to.

Remember that your principal reports regularly to the superintendent, and the superintendent reports regularly to the school board. There is nothing that goes on in your school that your principal will not hear about. He or she will most likely hear about anything involving the teachers, students, and the students' parents, which is why it is imperative that, above all, you maintain a professional appearance and manner at all times.

A Few Words on Excellent Administrators

CASE STUDY: TIPS FROM
VETERAN TEACHERS

Jennifer Sherrill
Second-grade teacher
Sunrise Elementary
Palm Bay, Florida

"I expect my administration to stand behind me in decisions that I make and I, in return, need to give them all the evidence that I was the best selection for my job."

Good teachers are the most important resource a principal has. Learning about administration and their responsibilities also makes you realize how important it is for teachers to have good administrators. Excellent administrators are essential to make a teacher's job enjoyable and successful. A teacher can be an effective mentor for their students without a good principal, but guiding your students is easier with a good leader in your school.

A good leader allows you to do your job without interference. He or she knows you have a job to do, believes in your ability to do that job, and allows you to do the job without looking over your shoulder. A leader must have heart and the ability to help those who come to you.

An excellent educational leader knows an effective teacher loves working with children and wants to see his or her students succeed more than anything. Good principals have faith in your sincerity and your abilities. They will be there for you, regardless of whether you need them.

If you have a concern or a problem, an excellent leader will take the time to hear your worries. He or she will know whether you simply need a sounding board, words of advice, or both. This is possible because a good principal will get to know you as a person — not only as a teacher. Another important quality a good principal will have is integrity. Not only is it necessary that the teacher loves working with children and has their students' success as their goal, but it is just as important for the principal to have the same personal qualities and goals. An honest, caring principal is essential for a school to be successful. Such a principal knows your value and cherishes you as a resource for the success of his or her school.

According to Melissa Kelly, a secondary education guide and writer for the Web site **www.About.com**, due to the stress and demands on a teacher, 20 to 30 percent of them leave the field within the first three years of starting their career; believe it or not, 9.3 percent of them do not even make it through their first year. It is also sad to report that almost 50 percent of the new teachers leave teaching after five years. The reasons for these statistics vary from raising their own children to the low pay and exhaustion of the job. Another reason many teachers leave is because of inadequate support from administration.

In order to have adequate support as a new teacher or even a veteran teacher, there needs to be a good relationship between the teacher and the administrator. It is critical that administrators support their teachers and ensure a positive learning environment in their schools. You want your administrator to have a moral purpose. He or she needs to understand the change process, listen to those who point out flaws in proposed changes, and adjust those changes accordingly. A good administrator will continuously strive to develop and nurture the relationships with his or her teachers, knowing the importance of those relationships. A good administrator will not buckle under the demands of politics and people in the community, but will remain focused on what should be the main goal: student learning.

Unfortunately, you as a teacher do not have the ability to change your school principal. This is why it is crucial, if at all possible, to learn about the principal of the school in which you are interested in teaching. As a new, incoming teacher, it is important to look for an accessible, respectful, supportive, and caring principal.

The significance of the relationship between administrators and teachers has become obvious to educational researchers, school administrators, and teachers over the years. Unfortunately, even if a school has all these assets and becomes a successful school, there are always politics involved.

Politics in Education

Control and funding for education in America comes from three places: federal, state, and local governments. The federal government has a large impact on how much funding schools receive because it sets the standards on how much money each district is allowed from federal funding. The state has a say in how much funding certain schools will receive from state funds.

No Child Left Behind

It is widely understood that the state and the school district now mandate the standards you cover in your classroom. These standards are set so your students can better meet the level the federal government set in the No Child Left Behind Act (NCLB). In 2002, NCLB was signed into law and passed with the intentions of getting all students' performances up to their grade level by the year 2014. The goal was having all students receive a quality education, regardless of race, geographic location, or nationality, and to be at a certain level of knowledge according to their grade.

Each state has their own way of attaining federal requirements when it comes to NCLB. An example of this is the Ohio Achievement Test (OAT). This test is given in grades three through eight, and the test is based on Ohio's Academic Content Standards. In high school, Ohio uses the Ohio Graduation Test (OGT) to assess students, and it is given in tenth grade. Those who do not pass the OAT or the OGT are allowed to retake the test, or certain sections of the test they do not pass, until all subject areas are passed. If the student does not pass all subject areas in the OGT before their graduation date, they are not allowed to receive their diploma. In Florida, the Florida Comprehensive Assessment Test (FCAT) is administered to students in grades three through 11. The test has criteria to be met in the subject areas of math, writing, science, and reading. The test is based on the Sunshine State Standards (SSS), which are benchmarks created by the state to meet the NCLB standards.

NCLB forces states to be accountable, and the accountability system is based on the development of state content and academic achievement standards. If the state wishes to receive NCLB funding, that state must meet federal standards that are set in reading/language arts, math, and science. The U.S. Department of Education allows each state to develop their own standards, assessments, and adequate yearly expectations, but said standards are reviewed by the U.S. Department of Education before and after testing.

This act requires assessments in different subjects at certain grade levels. These assessments are to be acquired during specified years set by the government. What does NCLB mean for elementary teachers? Because of this act, there are more responsibilities for teachers and administrators. A few of the new expectations and realizations for those who teach grades K-6 according to the NCLB are:

- All teachers who teach a core subject in a public school are required to be highly qualified. Under the federal law, teachers who do not teach a core subject area — such as physical education teachers, counselors, nurses, and librarians — are not required to be what is deemed as highly qualified. Those who teach core academic subjects — such as English, reading/language arts, art, theater, music, math, science, foreign languages, social studies, speech communications, history, economics, geography, civics, and government — must be highly qualified.

- Under NCLB, highly qualified means a teacher is fully certified with a bachelor's degree (no emergency certifications). The teacher must demonstrate competency in each academic core subject he or she teachers by doing one of the following:

1. Passing the state-approved elementary PRAXIS II exam

2. Scoring 100 points on the state's HOUSSE matrix

3. Receiving National Board Certification for grades K-3 as an Early Childhood/Generalist, for grades 3-6 as a Middle

Childhood/Generalist, or for Grade 6 as a Generalist/
Early Adolescent

4. Passing the State Performance Review

5. Stating reciprocity

- A master's degree does not qualify a teacher for a highly qualified designation

According to author Barnett Berry and the Teacher Leaders Network, evidence shows the majority of districts are spending more time on math and
reading, which forces teachers to neglect needed time on music, art, and
social studies. For the sake of raising test scores, some schools have eliminated recess, art, and music altogether. This worry of teachers having to
teach for state testing because of NCLB is the greatest challenge many new
teachers face. The enormity of what you are expected to teach in a year is
overwhelming; just remember that other teachers have been meeting those
expectations for some time now, and if they can do it, so can you. It is not
impossible, but it is frustrating and trying for teachers.

There are four mainstays of the NCLB:

- Accountability
- Flexibility in federal funding
- Scientifically based educational programs
- Certain rights for parents of students

When the federal government says a school is held accountable, they mean
what they say. Some of the sanctions for failing to meet NCLB standards,
according to the law, require schools to offer extra tutoring and allow
parents to transfer their children to higher performing schools. The extra
tutoring comes out of school budgets, forcing cuts elsewhere, which leads

to students doing even worse on state tests. When students do poorly on the standardized tests, schools begin facing a possible state takeover or another sanction, and administrators and teachers become desperate because it will mean losing their jobs. A school board does not want an administrator who cannot get his or her school to meet the set standards. The same is true for teachers, and they must also worry about job cuts, which come with a state takeover.

There were once stringent rules as to how public schools could spend federal funding. With NCLB, these rules are now more relaxed. Funds may now be spent with specific needs based upon a school's locality, such as more training for teachers. If a school district has a high ratio of teachers with special needs students, training is more crucial for these teachers. Training improves staff development and is therefore justified as needed.

NCLB allows parents other alternatives if their child is attending a low-performing school. Transferring a student is allowed if the school is deemed low-performing for two consecutive years. If the school is low-performing for three years, the parent may remove the child and place them in a better-performing school in the same district or receive supplemental services, such as tutoring.

According to the Civil Rights Project at Harvard University, educators at all levels are trying their best to implement the laws of NCLB, but for many it leaves a taste of aggravation and frustration. Even with the negative aspects, teachers do admit that the NCLB has forced states to give equal education to all students in the school system.

Frustration is common in students because of the possibility of not being able to be moved to the next grade level due to low test scores. Some students do not test well, and even those who do may have a bad day on test day. It should be noted that academically successful students in elementary school are looked at closely when it comes to having a bad test score, and exceptions do apply. Exasperation among teachers is also common when discussing NCLB. Veteran teacher Carol Baker knows that feeling first-hand, but focuses on what is most important.

CASE STUDY: TIPS FROM
VETERAN TEACHERS

Carol Baker
Third-grade teacher
Sunrise Elementary School
Palm Bay, Florida

"[No Child Left Behind] is a good theory," said Carol Baker. "Unfortunately, some students need to be in the environment where they will be successful and can build the knowledge at their pace, not just move on to the next level because the law tells them to. That is not going to make them understand math and how to read."

Baker believes students will just get more lost, and their confidence and self-worth will start to fade. "It is then up to the teacher to pull their resources to help the child in areas that are weak and try to build their confidence by allowing them to be successful on their level. Not that it is a burden on us as the teacher, but the student will always struggle and may not always get a teacher that will devote as much time and effort that is needed to make those children successful."

Baker said every career has superiors who make the rules but do not work in the field where these rules must be followed. "Bottom line: You make the best of it and remember that you are there for the students, and their best interest is what is important," she said.

In order to help your students pass the tests that show they have mastered the objectives the district and state outlined, you must first accept the importance of these standards. If you do not believe in the standards you are teaching, your teaching skills will be affected, you will not be the most effective teacher you can be, and your students will not do well on the mandated tests.

State-mandated tests

Each state must create standards that say what material your students will master by the end of the school year in order to pass to the next grade level; you, as a teacher, must design a course of study for your students to meet those standards. These standards can be found on every state's department of education Web site. This is the foundation of your lesson plans. Having your students master those standards should be your objective because this will be the gauge that determines whether your students are successful.

For elementary teachers, meeting state standards means being committed to your students and what they learn. What teachers know and do has the most impact on what their students will learn. The National Council for Accreditation of Teacher Education expresses that teachers must know more about the foundations of subject areas, and they must understand how students think, as well as what they know, to create experiences that produce learning.

Educators are being asked to master new skills in order to teach the state standards. The number of responsibilities teachers are expected to meet raises the bar even higher. According to the Consortium for Policy Research in Education (CPRE), when it comes to working with children, teachers need the opportunities to develop, master, and reflect upon their skills. The CPRE believes in the need for time and training for all teachers, especially elementary, because with state standards, there will have to be new approaches in how students are taught.

Be prepared to deal with complaints from parents when it gets close to time for the state-mandated tests. Some students do not test well; others will fly through the tests with no problem. Regardless, there are parents who resent these ordered tests, usually due to the students' stress and complaints.

In June 2009, a principal and assistant principal were arrested for cheating on students' standardized tests in Georgia, The principal resigned during the investigation after being accused of altering student tests. The assistant principal turned herself into authorities and was reassigned during the investigation process. At the time of the investigation, there were tests from schools in three other systems that were being reviewed. Both the principal and assistant principal were charged with altering public documents. When considering what the two administrators allegedly did, one must wonder what would push someone to do something this serious. The result of their test alterations sums up the answer: The resulting higher scores after the alterations helped four schools meet standards and avoid the sanctions the schools would have received due to NCLB.

While it is unfortunate you must adhere to state-mandated testing even if you know it is not good for your students, the good news is you have the freedom to create lesson plans that can teach what the students have to know in a way you do believe in. Principal Oliver Phipps of Estates Elementary School in Naples, Florida, said the biggest challenge he faces as an administrator is maintaining morale. "There is always something like lack of funding, paperwork to keep organized, dealing with so many tests, laws, changes … it's hard to keep upbeat and stay focused," he said. "Another problem is maintaining the state assessment grade," which are state-mandated tests used to measure student attainment.

When discussing standardized testing in the schools, Phipps had good advice: "Do not play [standardized tests] up. That is too much pressure on the kids and parents. Teach the standards and curriculum, and all will be fine."

Improvements through the years

Many people believe educational standards have diminished in our schools, but the truth is that there are many educational advancements that have been made in the educational system. It was only 55 years ago that the Supreme Court decision in *Brown v. Board of Education* began desegregation in the schools. Today, our schools give the same rights to all students, no matter their race, and this is a major improvement in the educational system.

Another change that has taken place in education due to politics: Female students are not as stereotyped and restricted as they once were. Girls were expected to take sewing classes while boys became lawyers. When women were granted equal rights, the view of girls in schools and the possibilities of what they could do started to change. No longer are girls pushed to take home economics while boys are expected to take shop class.

There was a time when teachers taught only one way. All students were expected to follow that method of teaching, and they either understood what the teacher taught or fell behind the rest of the class. Many times this method of one-way teaching had negative long-term consequences, which meant the student never caught up and just continued to fall further behind with each passing year. Today, prospective teachers are taught that different students learn in different ways. When teachers learn new methods of teaching for individual students, this ensures all students have a better chance of becoming better educated.

When elementary teachers talk about their class as a whole, they are usually referring to where their students are academically, and this directly dictates how a teacher will teach for the year. First, they assess their students with tests from books, standardized tests, or tests they create themselves. Once students have been assessed, the method of teaching is chosen. Some of the methods of teaching include:

- **Direct instruction** — This is the most common form of instruction and is a lecturing method of teaching. This is not best for elementary students who need a more hands-on approach.

- **Inquiry-based learning** — This takes more creativeness and lesson planning, but it has proved to be more effective. This method is student-centered and student-directed, allowing students to practice problem solving and critical thinking skills.

- **Cooperative learning** — A method where students are grouped together; these groups usually consist of students at different levels.

- **Information-processing strategies** — This method is best to use when facts need to be memorized. Facts and concepts can be grouped for better understanding. Using a variety of teaching methods can be intellectually stimulating, both for the teacher and the students, and it can keep children from becoming bored.

Inclusion

Another area in which politics and education have added stress and responsibilities on teachers is in the requirements on educating special needs students. In the mid-1960s, President Lyndon B. Johnson's "Great Society" programs included the Elementary and Secondary Education Act, which was an attempt to do away with poverty and racial injustice. A decade later, the U.S. Supreme Court enacted federal legislation — Individuals with Disabilities Education Act (IDEA) — that required states to ensure the same education for students with disabilities as those without disabilities.

After a number of federal and state laws were passed, school districts found themselves scrambling to provide services to students with exceptional needs. Bureaucratic rights have since been established protecting the rights of parents of special needs children so they have a voice in their children's education. Rights have also been established to protect the students and ensure their educational rights. What has come from these laws and rights is better known as inclusion. An inclusion classroom incorporates teaching special needs students in regular classrooms, eliminating the need for a special needs school whenever possible. Judgments for inclusion are said to be based on IDEA, which calls for educating children with disabilities in the least-restrictive environment.

In 1997, there were amendments made to IDEA that required schools to educate special needs children in regular classrooms whenever possible. This was when the requirement for all special needs children to have an Individual Education Plan (IEP) was put into place. By law, the IEP must be developed by a team of people that includes teachers, administrators, parents, councilors, and outside experts such as a psychologist who interprets the student's evaluation test and the instructional implications that will follow. The student for which the plan is developed is also part of the IEP team. Together, this team creates a learning plan that stresses the special needs of the child so their educational needs are met.

Agendas in schools had to be restructured to adapt to inclusion, and today the inclusion classroom is the standard classroom model. It took several years for teachers to receive necessary training for inclusion, and in some districts this lack of training is still a problem that has not been addressed. Today, teachers must be prepared to change the material they teach to adapt instructions for any special needs individual.

While it is true the challenge to create lesson plans that keep students interested can be particularly trying, this can be incredibly difficult for elementary students, especially when the teachers have to consider inclusion. What once would have been a class of minimal differences in academic levels now becomes a class with a broader spectrum of academic differences. Before inclusion was implemented, it would have been fairly easy to make your lesson plans and stick to them for the day. Now, on any particular day, there is a higher chance that one or two students may become disruptive, and that lesson plan will not work out. To avoid this possibility, an effective elementary teacher will plan more than what he or she expects to be accomplished. This way, if a particular part of the lesson plan is not working, you can switch to something different. Also, you may be pleased to find that your expectations are met.

It may seem to some people that the number of students with special needs is minimal, but approximately half the current population of the United States is affected by disabilities, either themselves or through association. The United States reported that in the school year 2006-2007, there were more than 6.6 million students between the ages of 3 and 11 with disabilities who were served in schools with non-disabled peers. Because of the increasing number of students with disabilities, there is a greater impact on teachers, as they must serve these students in classes with non-disabled students.

People who create learning programs for teaching degrees are now encouraged to change these programs to include inclusion concepts. An example of the inclusion concept would be a teacher's knowing how to deal with an autistic child. Without proper training, the teachers are at a loss. Teachers who have been successful with inclusion classrooms have said that resources, time, and training were the determining factors in their accomplishments. With inclusion being the standard in all classrooms, the concepts of teaching and learning must adapt for the benefit of both teachers and students.

States provide a minimum basic special education allocation. This funding is based on a per-pupil amount for a district's entire student population. Funds for special education services are distributed through Special Education Local Plan Areas (SELPA). Under certain circumstances, charter schools also receive funds through SELPA.

With decreased funding, teachers will find it more difficult to find resources to teach special needs students. Regardless of the burden brought on by budget cuts, inclusion is a law by which teachers must abide. Approximately half of the student population enrolled in special education is placed there due to having a learning disability. Approximately one-quarter of the special education students have a speech or language impairment that qualifies the students for extra assistance. The problem is these special needs students have a large impact on the cost of education. The even larger impact comes with the cost of educating the other quarter of those special needs students with more severe disabilities. Those disabilities with a more serious nature include visual, orthopedic, or other health impairments; mental retardation; emotional disorders; loss of sight and/or hearing; or multiple disabilities. In 2005-2006, regular education spending totaled less than $10,000 per pupil in elementary and secondary schools. According to the Center for Special Education Finance, the average spending on Special Education students totals between $20,000 and $30,000, depending on the state.

Another special needs area is English Learners, for which the U.S. Supreme Court established English Language Learners (ELL) rights by passing the Education Opportunity Act of 1974. School districts are now required to address linguistic deficiencies of language minorities. Unfortunately, the court failed to suggest any specific way in which the schools are to remedy the problem.

Through all of these state and federal requirements you must meet, remember that your administration is there to help you succeed. Your success is their success, and all of you are working together to achieve the same goal.

Federal involvement

You will see politics affecting education from incidents involving unions to incidents that reach the president. One example of such an incident is the big push for more involvement of teacher unions in the charter schools. Since President Barack Obama's administration began pushing for more charter schools, the teachers unions have reacted, wanting more of the charter schoolteachers to become unionized. In 2009, Education Secretary Arne Duncan began threatening to withhold millions of dollars in funding from states that put limitations on their charter schools. The unions reacted, seeing this as a way to get more of the charter schoolteachers in the union.

President Obama said he is working to find ways to ease the burden for teachers and at the same time improve the quality of education students receive. He is attempting to begin this process through his American Recovery and Reinvestment Act. On the official Web site of the Department of Education, **www.ed.gov/index.jhtml**, it is said that President Obama is "committed to providing every child access to a complete and competitive education, from cradle through career."

With the American Recovery and Reinvestment Act, there will be:

- $5 billion for early learning programs, including programs for children with special needs.

- $77 billion for reforms to strengthen elementary and secondary education, including $48.6 billion to stabilize state education budgets.

- $5 billion in competitive funds to spur innovation.

With the American Recovery and Reinvestment Act, $77 billion has been earmarked for reform to strengthen elementary and secondary education and is also to be used for encouraging states to "make improvements in teacher effectiveness and ensure that all schools have highly qualified teachers."

It has been said President Obama realized teachers are the most important resource to a child's learning, and he vows to ensure teachers are supported as professionals in the classroom. Claims to "use rewards and incentives to keep talented teachers in the schools that need them the most" have been made. This act offers new teachers promise and recognition, which many good teachers have never received. In February 2009, President Obama signed into law provisions of $98.2 billion in funding for the Department of Education. In March 2009, the president outlined five mainstays for reforming our schools in the budget request for the Department of Education. One of those mainstays includes recruiting, preparing, and rewarding effective teachers. For elementary teachers, two essential components of the budget request include:

- $370.4 million to expand the Striving Readers program to be used for children in elementary grades.

- $517.3 million for the Teacher Incentive Fund that includes, but is not limited to, financial rewards for teachers who improve student achievement.

On November 4, 2009, the White House released a statement on President Obama's commitment to reforming America's public schools. The release said he was presenting states with an "unprecedented challenge and the opportunity to compete in a 'Race to the Top' designed to spur systemic reform and innovative approaches to teaching and learning in America's schools." The Race to the Top challenge is backed by $4.3 billion dollars and expands effective support to teachers and principals.

Teachers as Role Models

Teachers are role models as well as educators in their classrooms. Due to the depersonalized ways of our society, teachers have found themselves needing to demonstrate social behavior for their students to learn. Skills such as common courtesy and mutual respect are lacking in some students because there is less interaction with people within our society, leaving teachers in a position that can make their classroom total chaos. Due to this possibility of disruption, teachers have started teaching social skills to their students. While it is one more thing for teachers to do, it is a blessing there is someone who is willing to do it. This change was brought about due to the schools realizing and addressing students' needs other than just curriculum needs. According to the National Association of School Psychologists (NASP), some social skills that students are able to learn from their teachers include:

- Anger management

- Recognizing others' point of view

- Social solving problem

- Peer negotiation

- Conflict management

- Peer resistance skills

- Active listening

- Peer communication

- Increased tolerance of diverse groups

There are many programs available for teachers to help students learn social skills. The NASP suggests that the Stop and Think program for schools is a good concept to use when teaching valuable, life-long social skills. These skills are narrowed down to:

- **Survival skills** — Learning how to follow directions, blocking out distractions, using language that is kind and brave, learning how to reward yourself

- **Interpersonal skills** — Sharing skills, asking for permission, participating in activities, learning to be patient

- **Problem solving skills** — Knowing when to ask for help, apologizing, accepting consequences, making wise decisions

- **Conflict resolution skills** — Teaching children how to deal with bullies, how to accept defeat, dealing with accusations, how to cope with feeling left out, coping with peer pressure

Coping With Budget Cuts

Many governors, senators, Congress members, and presidents have run their campaign on having better education in our states. However, as soon as the economy takes a downward turn, one of the first places that experiences cuts is education, which seems to be a trend most politicians follow. In 2006, President George W. Bush made a proposal to cut education spending by more than $3 billion dollars, but at the same time, he wanted to strengthen math and science programs. Many of the budget cuts came from scrapping education programs for the arts and state grants for vocational education, but in his State of the Union address, President Bush spoke of his focus on math and science by creating the American Competitiveness Initiative. This initiative included $250 million dollars for elementary programs to boost math achievement.

Since 2006, many states have been cutting budgets in education to find money they have lost with the closing of industries and other tax revenues. California once had an educational system that was claimed to be a national model. When Governor Arnold Schwarzenegger was planning to cut the education budget by $1.3 billion in the 2009 school year and $4 billion the following year, California schools would have drastically changed. However, in August 2009, Schwarzenegger stated the need for California to be eligible for the Race to the Top dollars available through President Obama's Recovery and Reinvestment Act. State legislators were on board to begin immediate work to reach this goal. The results will have long-term effects in California's educational system, and it is the administrators, teachers, and students who will either reap the rewards or pay the price.

Politicians are forcing schools to slash programs, lay off teachers, and expand class sizes to make up for money lost from other revenues. In Florida, a state that already struggles due to lack of funding, administrators were reported to say the budget cuts were "bleeding the education system." Students and teachers in central Florida rallied together and wore red shirts to represent their discontentment with the massive education budget cut of $100 million in February 2009. Governor Charlie Crist stated he was waiting for a waiver from the Secretary of Education to get the federal stimulus money for education. In February 2009, Florida was not eligible to receive the stimulus money because the state was not funding education enough to qualify, but they were allowed a waiver and had to make promises to the federal government to give more funding to education over the next several years. Due to the waiver and the state's promise, they did receive a small amount of stimulus funding, and Broward County was able to call back 100 of the 400 teachers they were forced to lay off, many of whom were elementary teachers. As of May 2009, the federal government did allow $599 million for education funds, and the state of Florida is eligible to apply for $891 million more in fall 2010.

The Kansas Legislature pursued a $26 million cut in K-12 funding due to a $680 million state deficit. Governor Kathleen Sebelius objected, pointing out that the state was expecting to receive $387 million in federal stimulus education aid.

In Ohio, some school districts will be receiving little or no additional money over the next two years under a new funding formula created by Governor Ted Strickland. However, Ohio education is due to receive a small stimulus package for Title 1 and Special Education programs. Title 1 is the largest federally funded program on record, and it covers supplemental funds for school districts with the highest number of students in poverty.

It seems each year brings new stress to teachers and administrators when it comes to budget cuts. In the 2009-2010 school year, many schools are feeling the effects of a bad economy regardless of the new funding from our federal Department of Education. In Forest Lake, Minnesota, elementary schools had their budget cut by $762,000. In Billings, Montana, the public school elementary grades face a $1.9 million shortfall for the 2010-2011 year. Even though the state will receive stimulus money from the federal government, the state is hesitant to use the one-time funding for regular operating expenses. In Orange County, California, the Capistrano Unified School will face the loss of more than half the district's guidance school counselors, 11 assistant principals, and an intervention program for elementary level students in the 2009-2010 school year.

When discussing state and federal mandates and/or budget cuts, the ties between politics and education can seem distant and impersonal, but there have been incidents that show just how close the ties between these two entities have become entangled. In June 2009, the governor of Ohio proposed a 50 percent budget cut for local libraries. For some libraries, state funding is where most of their money comes from. One example is the Fremont Public Library in Fremont, Ohio, which receives 81 percent of its funding from the state. If funding were cut 50 percent like the governor had planned, that would leave Fremont Public Library with 50 percent of the money they receive annually from the state and other resources combined. Thankfully, the proposal was rejected, and even though 31 percent of funding for libraries was cut, it was less than what the governor had initially proposed. Many low-income students depend on libraries for resources such as computers, Internet, and books for reports. The consequences of this proposed cut could affect much more than just libraries.

Hope for better education and resources for our teachers to better achieve their goal of student success does prevail. As in any educational facility, you will find achieving your goal to be a successful teacher is easier to attain with the help of your colleagues.

Working With Your Colleagues

As if new teachers do not have enough responsibility thrown on their shoulders, there is another silent set of rules that can make or break your career as a teacher: your colleagues' expectations. There are some districts that encourage a warm and welcoming environment, nurturing relationships between teachers. But other districts and schools do not have the time or interest in fostering relationships between grown men and women who may or may not get along. Regardless of which type of school you are working in, it is in your best interest to befriend your coworkers.

In all schools, there are a number of teachers, and this means a number of different personalities. Various personalities mean different opinions and ideas, which can easily lead to disagreements. There will also be character conflicts, cliques, and those whose idea of success means politicking or brown-nosing the administration. Anywhere someone works, there will be people who make the job easier and people who make the job harder. Regardless of the effect they have on you, these are the people you will be working with, and it is best to communicate with all of your colleagues. It is also important for you to befriend those you feel most comfortable with. Some points to consider when thinking about how to get along with your colleagues are:

- Knowing the importance of neutrality
- Having good attendance
- Working together
- Accepting diversity in your colleagues

The importance of neutrality

The best approach for a new teacher to take when getting to know his or her colleagues during that first year is to keep eyes open and opinions neutral. While sitting in the teacher's lounge or observing teachers for the benefit of learning new methods, say as little as possible and only as much as necessary. This is the best way to learn the political climate in your school, the most effective way to discover who the good teachers are, and even the most secure way to learn more about your administrators. It is also the safest way to be sure you do not make anyone angry.

You will want to communicate, but be sure to do so professionally. The last thing you need as a new teacher is to be labeled a gossip. Do not be cold and distant, but a bit on the quiet side and always professional. You are going to need to watch the staff, listen to the teachers, and observe their body language and words when they interact with one another. If you do this, you will be looked upon as a professional coworker and someone who can be trusted. Another advantage to sticking to this kind of behavior is teachers and staff will feel they can tell you their opinions and feelings, and this is how you will learn the peculiarities of your school.

Make sure you do not react dramatically to anything you are told. It is best to simply nod and smile, or say, "Really?" With these types of noncommittal responses, you will seem interested but will not say anything to involve yourself or get yourself into hot water with other teachers or administration. If Mr. Smith came to your room and told you that Ms. Hopkins was hoarding supplies and he does not know why because she is a horrible teacher and will never use them, it would be a good time to smile, nod, and excuse yourself to go to the restroom. Over time, you will also learn who the best administrative person is to go to for advice in curriculum, why certain teachers are avoided, and which teachers help one another with no questions asked.

Having good attendance

Another important consideration for new teachers is how their peers and supervisors view them. One thing a new teacher does not want to be known for is excessive absences or consistent tardiness. There will be meetings to attend, most likely faculty and district-wide meetings. These are meetings in which your attendance is required and expected, and it is in your best interest to make sure you attend all of them. Be sure to attend all staff meetings, and do not show up late. Arriving late is a sure way to get labeled as unreliable, and if your administrators see you as unreliable, they will not want to renew your contract.

It is at these meetings that you will learn even more about your colleagues, such as who the outspoken ones are, who the ones who complain are, and who the ones with the best sense of humor are. These meetings will also be informative on subject matter such as testing procedures, certification options, student problems, and more. Remember, the more information you gather in your first year, the easier the years that follow.

The meetings you attend are also a good way to share time with your coworkers, as well as where laughter, ideas, family, and school stories all abound. It is an opportunity to connect and learn more about one another, and a good time to come out of your room so you may socialize with your colleagues. These meetings are where you are once again a team, and as a team player, you will attend the meetings with a positive attitude.

Working together

Aside from the district-wide and school-mandated meetings, you will have other opportunities to bond with you fellow teachers. Lunchtime is an excellent time for teachers to vent to one another, and the teacher's lounge is a place where you will learn many things about your environment. Not only will you hear about the teachers' and administration's actions, but you will also pick up on different teaching techniques. Once you have listened and learned who the effective teachers are, you will find the lounges are exceptional places to soak up everything those great teachers have to say. The teacher's lounge is the gathering place for teachers to update one another on everything from what the assistant superintendent has said to when the next staff meeting will take place. Join in the fun and the small talk about the weather, new books, and any local events, and you will be viewed as a team player. Most likely, this is the place where you will be invited to join your peers in a number of activities.

Teacher gatherings are something that take place often because many teachers seem to love to throw parties on a regular basis. When invited, your first thought might be that you do not have the time. However, it is in your best interest to make the time and use these opportunities. The fact that these social gatherings are where teachers open up the most can be advantageous to you as a new teacher.

These functions are also a good way to socialize and familiarize yourself with your colleagues and your community. You will learn about which parents are the most active with their schools and which ones are not involved at all. This is the place where you will hear about community events, both those that have already taken place and those that will be taking place. Due to limited time and work overload, you do not need to attend every social gathering you are invited to, but it is good to attend at least a few each year. In time, you will decide which ones you do not want to miss.

Participating in faculty-sponsored events is a positive trait, but attempting to do too much is not. It is all right to decline every now and then. If your plate is already full, politely decline, explain that you cannot possibly take part, and excuse yourself from participating adequately. If you attempt to do too much, it will affect your performance in the classroom and your students' success, which is your main priority. It is why you took this job in the first place, so you do not want to do anything to ruin that achievement. Remember, it is acceptable to say no when there is none of you left to share.

Be very cautious whom you confide in, at least until you are sure of your colleagues. Do not participate in rumors or gossip; this is the fastest way to get a bad reputation and ruin any chance of having a good relationship with your coworkers.

You might find there are issues between coworkers in your school. This is common and as stated previously, character conflict is to be expected. Your best bet is to stay out of it. If a colleague comes to you and starts complaining about another colleague, do not join in. Try to cut the conversation short and get away from that coworker as this is most likely one of the coworkers you will wish to have minimal contact with. When there are many personality types in one building, it is almost impossible to avoid issues between colleagues.

Accepting diversity in your colleagues

Each person you work with will bring his or her individual personality and teaching beliefs to work each day. It is your job — as well as the job of your administration and colleagues — to learn how to work with each other. Some teachers will be willing to offer you assistance in any way that they can, but other teachers will not be as generous. Another personality type you will wish to avoid is the negative teacher. These people find the worst in all people and situations, spouting their negativity everywhere they go. The biggest drawback about these people is how they pull others down with them. Negativity is contagious, but in your chosen career it is important you remain upbeat and positive. If at all possible, avoid the negative teacher and have as little contact with that person as possible. If negative Mr. Smith is in the room next to yours and you find yourself in a situation where you must deal with his consistent pessimism, you will bode well to close the classroom door when your class is not there. If closing the door is not enough, try purchasing or making a Do Not Disturb sign and hanging it in plain view. Be sure you do not give Mr. Smith feedback, because this will only encourage his visits. You could always excuse yourself to prepare lessons or explain you need to speak with the secretary, or perhaps this would be a good time to return phone calls. If absolutely necessary, you may have to tell Mr. Smith that you try very hard to keep a positive attitude for yourself and your students, and you prefer to have conversations that are not negative.

You will find that some schools have teachers who see themselves as the coach of all teachers because they are a sports coach, and some of these teachers would rather coach than teach. These types of teachers usually have other teachers who resent them because of assumptions that they care more about sports than academics, and that they get more breaks and support than the other teachers. In some cases this is true, but that entirely depends on what kind of leader your school principal is. Regardless of whether it is true, you will likely find there is tension between the coaching teachers and the academic-only teachers. It is best to avoid this conflict and make your own personal conclusions about what kind of teacher the coach is.

Sometimes you might find a grouchy, bitter teacher in your building. These teachers usually have been teaching a very long time and, for one reason or another, they never grew beyond the disenchantment stage of the profession. These are the teachers who sit in the lounge or at teacher gatherings and do nothing but complain. Avoid these people whenever possible.

Every building has a favorite teacher among the students. They love this teacher and compare every other teacher in the school to him or her. Do not feel bad about falling short when compared to the school favorite. In time, you may approach this teacher and ask what his or her secret is. It is also possible that once the students get to know you, you will also become one of their favorites. For now, you are new, and it is going to take some time to get yourself situated. The best way to reach your students is to talk to them about something personal in your life and listen when they talk to you about something personal in their life. Talk about something funny that happened the previous evening or a play that you went to see. Even if you take only five minutes at the beginning of the day, kids appreciate this personal time with their teacher. This kind of time creates a common and mutual respect for one another as people.

Do not be afraid to ask your colleagues for help. Most likely there will be at least one teacher who will dislike you from the moment he or she hears that you have been hired. This attitude may develop due to a personality clash, or the attitude may develop before he or she even meets you or knows anything about you, simply because you are new. Obviously, this is not the person you want to approach if at all possible. It is possible, though, that this is the very teacher who has the answer to your question. If that is the case, approach him or her with respect, but be cautious. Remember that some people develop attitudes with no rhyme or reason, and it is best to not take it personally. There have been teachers who started their new job in a school, and the teacher who has an attitude toward them turns out to be the liaison for their department. Under these circumstances it will be a very hard year for a new teacher and, regardless of what he or she does or does not do, the veteran teacher may never give them the opportunity to prove their value. If, by chance, you find yourself in such a situation, it would be wise to start looking for a new job when your contract is close to ending. Meanwhile, you will need someone to talk to about your frustrations.

On the other hand, if you are offered help from a colleague, accept it. This teacher may have years of experience from which you can learn many things. Not only would it be rude to turn down an offer of help, but you may be shortchanging yourself on what could possibly be a golden opportunity to learn.

In this first year, it is important that while you are trying to do everything from lesson planning to focusing all your energy on your students, you do not forget to spend time with the adults in your building. Although creating friendships with other teachers takes more time and effort than bonding with your students, it is important that you do so. Having someone to talk to about job frustrations is healthy, and this will help you have a better chance of surviving the year with your sense of humor still intact.

Do not define yourself on how different you are from your coworkers. If you do this, your colleagues will pick up on it and feel you are judging them. First of all, it is much too early in your career for you to judge your coworkers. Second, most likely they have been teaching a lot longer than you have. It is only natural that veteran teachers do not handle criticism from rookies very well.

There is another group of people in your building that you need to pay attention to, and they are an important asset for your school. Let us talk about those people and discuss why they are so important. A good name for this group is the "moral fiber of the school."

The Moral Fiber of Your School

Have you ever walked into an elementary classroom after all the students and the teacher have gone home? Have you ever seen an elementary classroom after a craft project or a science project? It is especially interesting to see this after one of these projects has run late and the students must hurry to put their belongings away before running to get on the bus in time. You will often find small pieces of paper, scissors, glue, pencils, and various objects all over the floor.

Have you ever entered a lunchroom after all the students in the building have eaten and are back in their classrooms? Children are messy eaters, no matter their age. Even adults can be untidy and lazy when it comes to picking up after themselves. It can be surprising the mess people, young and old alike, leave behind after they eat.

While it is true teachers are some of the most unappreciated people in the world, there is another group of people who are more underappreciated: the support staff in your building. Take a moment and imagine how hard your job would be without the custodian to clean up those small bits of paper. He or she is the one who picks up the scissors and pencils, and cleans the glue off the desktops. What would it be like to not have that person clean your room or the restrooms on a daily basis? What would the cafeteria be like without the custodian?

The secretary, custodian, teacher's aide, and the kitchen staff have numerous duties, and they perform those duties efficiently every day. Without them, your school would be in total chaos, and your job would be impossible.

While you are forming relationships with the other teachers and taking the time to get to know them, do not forget the staff members. Learn their names and take the time to talk with them. Be kind and respectful, and let them know you recognize the importance of the duties they perform. Remember this particular group of people is part of the school team, and they play just as big a part in making sure the school mission and goal is being met.

The secretary

The secretary performs tasks that no one else would want to have to do. Imagine having a sick or angry student sitting in a chair and glaring at you for long periods of time while you are trying to do your job. Some schools do not have a nurse in-house, and this responsibility becomes one of the many tasks a secretary might perform. It is up to him or her to keep an eye on such students while they are waiting for their parent to arrive or for the principal to have the time to speak with them. He or she answers the phones, carries messages to the appropriate person, types letters, hands out medicine if the school does not have its own nurse, answers hundreds of questions, and does word processing for hours on end each day. He or she must have a smile on his or her face and be polite to a number of people who enter the office regardless of what kind of day he or she is having. This madness he or she deals with every day can be trying and nonstop, and yet he or she is there to make your and the principal's life easier. He or she is there for the students, the administration, and the parents. There are times he or she must deal with the media, and he or she does so with caution and finesse.

A secretary hears more about every person who is involved in your school than any person would want to hear. He or she catches all the gossip, all the complaints, deals with the parents who come in and scream at the principal or the teacher, and yet he or she smiles and does his or her job, never divulging all that he or she hears, and keeping the fast pace of multi-tasking. The secretary is someone you want to know and be kind to because he or she can make your life much easier and be an endless support system for your job.

The custodian

The custodian is the one who keeps your building maintained and running efficiently. Be sure to introduce yourself to this person because he or she will be especially important to you. Always acknowledge his or her presence when you see him or her. Custodians are usually the most ignored people in the building because, unfortunately, some teachers see them as hired help and treat them as though they are not as important as other staff members.

Most teachers are aware that their students should be made to clean up after themselves, but there are days with events, such as the late science project, when it is almost impossible. When this happens, be sure to explain to the custodian you ran out of time and apologize for this occurrence. Be respectful, and he or she is more likely to take good care of your needs.

The teacher's aide

If you have an aide or assistant count your blessings. This person is there to make your life easier, but that does not mean you should take advantage of him or her. Do not use him or her to do the jobs you dislike; he or she has enough to do without picking up your slack. It is important you appreciate him or her and realize what they do to help you and your students. Be polite, kind, and appreciative, and he or she may try to make your life easier.

An aide will work every day to help make your job easier and the students more comfortable in their environment. With that in mind, remember him or her as an important asset who, unfortunately, usually receives less respect and appreciation than you do. Show him or her you do realize his or her importance by thanking him or her and telling him or her how much he or she helps you. It is also a good idea to ask the students to thank your aide. Teachers can have their students make thank-you cards, draw pictures, or write stories of how the teacher's assistant has helped them in the classroom. Perhaps a smiling student handing a bouquet of flowers or a gift certificate to the teacher's aide would be an idea you can use to thank your aid. Also, small plants or flowers can be bought and containers for them decorated, giving the children an art project while also teaching them about appreciating someone who is important in their education.

The kitchen staff

If you have children or younger siblings, you understand how kids can become cranky when they are hungry. Students are growing, and this keeps them hungry most of the time. Thankfully, there is the kitchen staff that prepares lunches each day. Some schools now offer breakfasts for students as well, and the kitchen staff is always there to do the job. Lunchtime is also when you get a break, taking your lunch to the teacher's lounge, and it is another reason to be thankful for the kitchen staff. Imagine how taxing it would be if you had to monitor the students daily while they had their lunch. Be sure to thank the kitchen staff every time you get your lunch. It is also good to take the time to speak with them, showing genuine interest in them individually to show respect and gratitude.

Making a class card for the kitchen staff at holiday time is a good way to show appreciation and teach the class respect. As an individual, teachers should include the kitchen staff when handing out cards for the holidays. If you get to know the kitchen staff personally, you will eventually become aware of their special days, such as a birthday or anniversary. Take the time to wish them a happy birthday, showing them you care and appreciate what they do.

Understanding your surroundings at your new school is a good way to ease your nervousness about starting your career as a teacher, but being prepared will make it even better. Being prepared will be a large step in being successful.

Part Two:

Being a Prepared Teacher

"I am constantly assessing my children after skills and lessons are taught; that way, I know if I have to re-teach a certain item. I have mapped out my curriculum for the year and make sure that it is following state standards and everything is being covered."

— *Malia Jarvis, kindergarten teacher at Shumaker School in Bellevue, Ohio*

Chapter 4
Your New Role

You have chosen a noble career that can have a profound impact on our society. When you consider that you may be teaching our world's future leaders, it can be an intimidating thought. Taking these possibilities into consideration, you can now see why it is so important for you to be a positive role model and influence for so many young minds.

As a new teacher you will have concerns, and it may help to know all teachers do. In the case study below, Don Shinton, a fourth-grade teacher, shares what his greatest fear was when he started his job as a teacher.

CASE STUDY: TIPS FROM VETERAN TEACHERS

Don Shinton
Fourth-grade teacher
Cheston Elementary
Easton, Pennsylvania

CLASSIFIED CASE STUDIES

directly from the experts

"My greatest fears were being unable to motivate the students to learn. Especially in your first year, your students do not know who you are, so they are going to challenge you. You must be prepared to handle a lot of situations. I had no idea there were so many things the children would look to me for guidance. I was not sure that I would be able to keep up with the demands that were asked of me."

The fact, is you will never face a more important undertaking than the one you are about to experience. While it is true there are many demands, and the responsibilities are extreme, it is also true that teaching elementary students can be full of small, unexpected gratifications for many years to come.

Now that you have the job, you are going to be tossed into your classroom and left on your own to survive or fail. As author and teacher W. Michael Kelley said, "Teaching your first class based on what you learned in college is like being asked to swim across the Atlantic Ocean with nothing more than those little inflatable armbands." College gives you a good basis for some of the teaching job, but there are so many demands and intricacies that are not touched upon in college because there are too many scenarios and possibilities to teach. Kelley said in regard to the first year of teaching, "You will stay afloat, but you will swallow a lot of water along the way."

With all this said, it is time to begin planning for your first year as a teacher so it will be a successful one.

Tips For Planning Your Classroom

After you have read the files on your students; learned some things about your community; and you have met your principal, your colleagues, and some of the school staff, it is time to prepare your classroom for your first year of teaching. Shortly before school begins, you will have many meetings to attend, and this will limit the time you have available to prepare your classroom. Because of this, you may need to spend some time on the evenings and weekends preparing your room, but this will be time well-spent.

Until you put your own unique mark on your classroom, it is a shell with a teacher's desk, many student desks, and a chalkboard or whiteboard. You will want to decorate your room but not make it the typical apples and numbers. Put your touch on it, and be sure it is comfortable and inviting for yourself and your students. Some items you can put in your room could be plants, family pictures, pictures of pets, or some craft you made or had made for you. Your students will like the personal touch because it tells them more about you. This also helps with making conversation and helps to build a good relationship with your students. Some ideas for planning your classroom into a comfortable atmosphere for you and your students are:

- Utilize your bulletin boards
- Decide where to place desks
- Organize your space

Utilize your bulletin boards

If you have bulletin boards, you will want them to be creative and informative. If you are lucky, you will have two bulletin boards, one creative and the other informative. You might want to remember that some students are primarily visual learners, so a bulletin board reflecting what you are teaching is a good idea.

One suggestion is changing the bulletin board periodically and having the students as the main attraction. Some Parent Teacher Organizations (PTOs) have appointed members to attend school events and take pictures of the students, and you can place these on your bulletin board. Using pictures of your students for the bulletin board also creates a sense of community.

You may want your bulletin board to encourage competition by keeping score of the games your class plays, such as spelling games or math flashcards. This gives students encouragement and also teaches them the concept of competing.

You may also consider allowing the students to come up with themes of their own and having them craft decorations for the board. If you are really creative, you can figure ways to help the students work the present unit of lessons into the theme for the bulletin boards. If your class is studying plants and how they make their own food, create a bulletin board with pictures of plants, a display of how they absorb food from the sun and rain, and where they store it.

Decide where to place desks

Arranging the desks is important not only for the students' comfort, but also for traffic flow. Will you want to have interest centers, such as a quiet place for reading? Where will you want your desk to be placed? These are decisions you will want to make before school starts. Most teachers advise arranging desks in rows or in a horseshoe/double horseshoe so it is easy to see what your students are doing, eliminating a majority of horseplay. It is also important none of your students have their back to you, especially when you are instructing them. Most likely, you will make changes in the seating arrangements when you get to know your students better.

You will probably want to leave an empty seat or two in the desk arrangement for students who start school late or transfer out. Families are more mobile today, and many students could come and go throughout the school year. Other considerations are air flow and temperature. When arranging the desks, you also need to think about noise from the hallway or windows and lighting. It will be important to keep the door area clear so students and parents can get in and out of your classroom in the mornings, when school lets out for the day, and during special events.

Once you decide where you want your own desk placed, you will want to make sure you have what you need in your immediate area. Even though you will spend little time at your desk other than at the beginning and the end of the day, you still want it to be placed where you can easily observe the whole room. You might want it placed close to the chalkboard or whiteboard, but some teachers do not see this as necessary.

Items you will need at your desk are important for your convenience. The following is a list of some of the items you may want to have nearby:

- Scissors
- Ruler
- Pens and pencils
- Paper clips
- File folders for each student
- Tape
- Stapler and staples
- Letter trays
- Notebook or file cards with students' names, parent or guardian names, and emergency numbers
- Sticky notes
- Note pad
- Hole punch
- Correction fluid
- Change for vending machines or lunches
- Highlighters
- Thumbtacks
- Tissues

Now that you have your desk placed, your students' desks or tables arranged, your room decorated, and your bulletin boards looking lively, colorful, and inviting, let us make sure the rest of your needs are in place for your room.

Organize your space

Arranging the rest of your room should be fairly easy once you have reached this point. If you have a filing cabinet, you may want to keep that item close to your desk for easy access unless you do not expect to use it very often. For other large items you may have, such as a long table, bookshelves, or storage bins, you should try to position them in terms of use. *In the Resources section of this book, you can find Web sites that share user-friendly layouts for teachers.*

You may want to create learning centers in your classroom. Dividing your room into separate areas will help keep you more organized.

Learning centers

Melissa Kelley, an experienced author and teacher, suggests elementary teachers think of four to six tasks you and your students will complete that require supplies then assign a location for each task. An example of one task would be reading six books in a grading period. You would want numerous books for the students to choose from, but they would need to be in an area that the students can get to easily, out of the way of normal traffic. Another example would be art projects; a large table would be handy for these if you have enough room.

If you plan to have learning centers, you can use tables, counters, large throw pillows, or a rug for these. You probably learned of the three types of learning methods while in school: visual, auditory, and kinesthetic. You can use a television for a visual center and a CD player for the auditory center.

The kinesthetic learner will most likely prefer objects they can manipulate with their hands — pattern blocks, cards, fraction bars, or play money. The learning centers can be used as incentives for the students. These centers give them the freedom to choose learning fields they prefer and also teaches them to work independently.

There are many ideas for centers of interest. Some of these ideas include:

- Science centers
- Reading areas
- Writing centers
- Audiovisual centers
- Math areas
- Computer center
- Game center
- Pet centers

Children love animals, and you could easily have an area with fish, birds, snakes, hamsters, mice, or guinea pigs. A pet center is an especially good idea because it can be used as an incentive, a resource for teaching responsibility, and a science center for learning about animals and animal behavior. If you have a pet center, remember to pay attention to the temperature in your room and placement of cages in regard to heat and sunlight.

Whatever you decide to place in your room and however you decide to arrange it, it is your world to create as you please. Make it an exciting and inviting room where your students will feel welcomed and loved.

Lesson Plans For Your Students

Every teacher has his or her own unique way of teaching and creating lesson plans. These lesson plans are important in helping ensure your students will learn the curriculum set by your school district and state.

Trying to meet the curriculum standards can be overwhelming, especially for a new teacher, but there are ways to meet the curriculum without overburdening yourself and your students. While some school districts are very clear about the curriculum you are to follow, other districts are not. If your district is one that clearly expresses what you are to teach and when you are to teach it, then be sure to get a copy of these materials and follow the set plan they have made for you. This next case study contains ideas for creating lesson plans and meeting state standards.

CASE STUDY: TIPS FROM VETERAN TEACHERS

Carol Baker
Third-grade teacher
Sunrise Elementary School
Palm Bay, Florida

Merrisa Herman
First-grade teacher
Shumaker Elementary School
Bellevue, Ohio

"[Teachers need to] know the standard of the subject and follow what you need to have the students understand," Carol Baker said. "From there, I can correlate my lesson plans with the standard to the activity I will then teach."

Merrisa Herman said she met with other first-grade teachers and received a lot of ideas from them. "I had several copies of the state standards, and I used those to create lessons, and I checked them off when that standard was taught and assessed. I used the teacher's manuals that were given to me to find lessons that went with state standards, and I tweaked those that didn't. I found a lot of different lessons using the Internet."

Herman also said she does a lot of hands-on activities for her students. "I have learned over the years that hands-on activities keep the students motivated and interested in what I am teaching. For example, this is my second year using an interactive whiteboard in my classroom. My students love to use it and get excited about what they are learning, and are more attentive during the lesson. I also try to do a variety of different activities and try to get my students moving throughout the day. First-graders have a very short attention span, so I try to change activities often."

Some teachers and administrators make overhead transparencies of this material so they can write in the updates as they take place. These teachers then use the transparencies to explain to the parents what their child will be learning. This is also an easy way to track, show, and explain any changes in the curriculum. Changes, or reform, in curriculum are very common and happen often due to the state and federal officials' attempts at making education better, so you may want to prepare for this in your first year by making the transparency copies.

As you plan your daily lessons, you will want to keep in mind the school calendar. School breaks from a normal routine will affect the flow of learning in your classroom. When students are on winter or spring break, some things they have learned prior to the first day of break will be lost; therefore, you should plan your lessons around your school calendar.

In a traditional school, you will have 180 days to teach your class, but on average you will lose approximately 30 of those days due to assemblies, special events, visits from firefighters and other local volunteers, or other interruptions. It may be easier if you organize your lesson plan as a unit plan. Take each unit and break it down into daily lessons by doing the following:

- Identify your objectives
- Determine what materials you will use to teach said objectives
- Plan alternatives for absent students, especially if your lesson plan can be hard to make up
- Decide how you will assess your students on these lesson plans

Consider your calendar with all school breaks marked off, then pencil in when your units of teaching will begin. This way, you will be able to use your calendar when writing your lesson plans in your plan book.

By taking the time to determine the objectives you want your students to learn, you will find you are reaching your set curriculum in a more organized way. Some schools ask their teachers to follow guidelines the federal government publishes. If this is the case, they will let you know in your meetings. In planning your daily lessons, you will also want to remember the state-mandated testing that takes place in your school.

Preparing for state-mandated tests

Some teachers feel a need to prepare their students for state-mandated tests. Other teachers feel that as long as their plans meet the curriculum requirements, the students are already learning what they need to know for the tests. Unfortunately, there are times the state-required testing does not reflect the curriculum your district sets. This can cause teachers to feel they need to not only cover the curriculum in their class, but also prepare students for the tests. If you feel your students need to be taught certain objectives before taking the state-mandated tests, you may want to shorten some lesson plans so you can lengthen the ones that teach the areas they will need to spend more time on.

Some school districts require you list the standards met on every lesson plan you use, which is another good reason to list your objectives for your lesson plans. For ideas on how to more effectively teach the material in your district, you can go to the National Board for Professional Teaching Standards at **www.nbpts.org**.

Crafting your lesson plans

You will find that with all you have to do in one day, there is not nearly enough time to prepare for tomorrow's lesson plan, but you can make your lesson plan brief and use your own personal shorthand when doing so. Some school districts require their teachers to turn in their lesson plans; if this is the case for you, you may want to add a few lines of explanation. Most schools do not mind brief plans as long as they are understandable in the hands of a superior.

How you write your daily lesson plans is up to you. While some teachers will write out their lesson word for word, others will use one to five sentences and naturally fill in the gaps while teaching the class. Whichever style is best for you is fine as long as you know the material and can answer questions your students ask. It is all right to be surprised by a question you have no answer for and learn the answer to that question with your students, but if you do not know the material and have no answers, you are going to look bad, lose the respect of your students, and be an ineffective teacher.

There are as many types of lesson plans as there are potential lessons. Certain elements, however, remain standard. Good lesson plans should include the following:

Title: What is the lesson about? Provide a title that is self-explanatory. You may know everything about the lesson now, but you may not remember it in the future. As the years progress, you will add to or change these titles accordingly.

Lesson plan identifier: Use a date or corresponding text. This number provides you with something for easier organization and identification later on.

Curriculum areas: What areas of the curriculum correspond to this lesson plan? What standards can be applied? Make sure you leave room for curriculum changes. You will also expand your knowledge with time and make changes to improve lesson plans in correspondence to the curriculum.

Objectives: This area of the plan relates to the standards and requirements that must be achieved based on school, state, and national guidelines.

Prior assessment: Before introducing any new material, you must understand your students' prior knowledge on the subject.

Teacher input: Plan what information you must provide to the students during the lesson.

Student activities: This area includes detailed descriptions of your specific plans for the students. Include information on the type of activity, such as whole group, small group, or individual activity.

Materials: Plan what materials you and the students will need. You will want to write where materials may be found. These ideas will come at different times, so be sure to have this close your desk.

Assessment: Provide different types of assessment for each lesson. This ensures that you will have sufficient information from the different types of learners.

In the first year of teaching, the lesson planning is the most time-consuming part of your job. Once you have lesson plans created, the planning in the following years will be easier because you can look back and adjust the plans you previously used. This will also make the job of grading papers and creating assessments easier in the future. At the end of the next section is a worksheet for young students that can be used for assessment. Making worksheets is easy with technology and free art clips on the Internet.

Common planning errors made by new or inexperienced teachers

Despite the amount of time spent on lesson planning in college or how many sample lesson plans you may reference, most new teachers are unprepared for the reality of this type of planning. It takes time, thought, energy, focus, and concentration, and even the most experienced teachers will have lesson plans fall apart for one reason or another. Here is a list of common lesson plan mistakes that often occur to first year teachers.

1. Forgetting the importance of writing course, unit, and daily plans in entirety and thinking they can "wing it" once they get into the classroom. A prepared teacher is a more effective teacher.

2. Despite the importance of mandates, ignoring or inadequately preparing for national, state, and district standards.

3. Mistakenly preparing only a list of activities instead of a full-fledged lesson plan.

4. Lecturing non-stop to the students for the entire lesson and forgetting to incorporate other elements, such as hands-on activities students can participate in.

5. Moving over the material too quickly, forgetting that many students need to be taught in different ways.

6. Eliminating elements that provide for different learning styles.

7. Forgetting to make provisions for adaptations.

8. Spending too much time on one aspect of the lesson or unit.

9. Forgetting to assess the prior knowledge base of the class and individual students before starting a lesson. This creates problems if a piece of the necessary knowledge base is missing. It also prevents the teacher from helping the students to make connections with previously learned material.

10. Failing to use elements that evoke critical thinking skills from the class.

11. Inadequately preparing the students prior to testing students.

12. Forgetting to provide sufficient practice opportunities for using the material.

13. Neglecting to prepare required materials ahead of time.

14. Forgetting to sufficiently fill out lesson plans that a substitute could easily follow.

Sample assessment

Directions: Circle the answer that matches the picture, then write the answer below each picture.

DOG CAT BIRD

_____

BLACK WHITE PINK

_____

COW BIRD GORILLA

_____

SWIMS CRAWLS HOPS

_____

ONE TWO THREE

_____

WHALE CAT FISH

_____

15. Eliminating homework and other assessment opportunities that help students master the material prior to testing.

Grading Papers and Creating Assessments

It is important to evaluate the students' understanding of the material you teach. Lesson plans and assessments go hand in hand, and keeping up with both is how administration will determine if you are doing your job. It is entirely possible for the principal to stop in and ask to see your lesson book. If this happens, you certainly want to be prepared. It is also possible that Megan's mom will stop in or call you out of the blue and ask why her grades have dropped. If you do not have assessments and are not prepared to pull Megan's file to show her where the problem is, she is going to think you are an ineffective and unqualified teacher.

Sometimes new teachers are hesitant to quiz or question the students on the lesson because they feel it breaks the flow of learning. While it is not necessary to quiz or question after every daily lesson plan, it is imperative that you do so enough to see how your students are doing.

There are two important things to remember when assessing students:

- One paper assignment in each class every day can mean anywhere from 150 to 900 papers to grade in a week, depending on where you teach and how many classes you teach in a day.

- It is not fair to overburden your students with homework, papers, and quizzes to make your job of doing assessments easier. There are better methods, such as answering review questions in class, and your students can be overwhelmed by work, just like you. They need their free time and family time, too.

Authors Jack Warner and Clyde Bryan advise teachers to skim over two of the papers handed in by students and correct every third paper in detail. They explain this will give an accurate assessment of the students' work.

There are many methods of assessing what your students have learned and the following are some examples:

- Recitals
- Drawing pictures or murals
- Verbal question and answer
- Group projects
- Classroom plays or finger painting
- Using or creating flash cards

Using alternative methods to evaluate what your students have learned breaks the monotony for them and for you, which is especially important for younger students. For example, if you create a play or take a story from a book to create a short play, you can assess student participation and see how much the student understands, listens, and responds while taking part in the play.

In the following case study, three veteran teachers share their ideas for creating assessments for your students.

CASE STUDY: TIPS FROM VETERAN TEACHERS

Don Shinton, Fourth-grade teacher
Cheston Elementary
Easton, Pennsylvania

Merrisa Herman, First-grade teacher
Shumaker Elementary School
Bellevue, Ohio

Jennifer Sherrill, Second-grade teacher
Sunrise Elementary
Palm Bay, Florida

"My assessments are created based on the state standards that need to be attained and the material that is covered during the lessons that are taught," said Don Shinton.

Jennifer Sherrill uses an assessment checklist throughout the year and suggests that teachers test each student individually with various tasks to see where they are academically. "The important thing to remember is to ask the questions that get right to the matter of what you are looking for," she said. She advises that "if you do not want to grade 'fluff and stuff' answers, then do not ask 'fluff and stuff' questions."

Merrisa Herman said she uses the computer to create a lot of her assessments: "I choose the skills that I feel the students should know, and then I use the computer to create an assessment that assesses that skill/concept. I also get ideas and assessments from other first-grade teachers. We use a lot of the same assessments," she said.

Remember: Your students need to know you care. While it is acceptable to only correct but not grade every paper, it is also important the students get feedback on their work. Throwing a red mark on a paper with no comment or words of encouragement will eventually make Tristan feel he is doing poorly. If you mark something as incorrect, take an extra minute to give a word of encouragement on something that is improving or is done very well. This will make a world of difference in the morale of your class.

Another method of gathering assessments to consider is student self-assessment. This is especially good to use with elementary-age students because it helps them learn as well as helps them be critical of their work and give them a different perspective of their work. While student self-assessment might be difficult to do with kindergartners or first-graders, it can be fairly easy to do with the other elementary grades. Younger students could copy a sentence or two you put on the chalk board to practice writing and spelling skills. Older students could copy a paragraph on material they have just learned. The paragraph will have blanks for the students to fill in with the correct answer. When the students are finished, you can write the correct version on the board and have them examine how they did in comparison. Depending on the age group, you could do this with spelling, writing, and any other subject area, putting your creativity to work.

Peer assessment is used by some teachers, sometimes because it is part of the curriculum and sometimes because the teacher feels it is good for the students to practice social skills. The biggest drawback in peer work is the good students' having to do the work of students who are lazy or have no motivation. One way to alleviate this problem is to break the assignment into segments and assign a part to each student. You can then grade the students for their individual sections without having to dock points from good students for the lack of effort of one or two students.

If you decide to use peer assessing, you should decide the criteria on which you will assess the work of the students, and tell them how they will be grading one another. Let the students know they will have to justify the grades they give their peers. Once you have assessed the project, both as a whole and in segments, you can give the students the job of assessing one another. This method of assessment is better for older elementary children such as grades four through six.

Calculating grades

Even though grading papers is part of the job, it does not have to be a burden that is carried home with you every night. It is a good idea to stay after school to do grading rather than take it home, but be sure to give yourself a cut-off time and stick to it. There is a possibility you will find time to do some grading during the day, perhaps during the students' library visit or during recess. No matter when you decide to do your grading, never allow yourself to do it during lunch. Lunch time is well-deserved and needed down time, and it is time for shop talk with your colleagues.

When you prepare the grade cards for your students, be sure to use the comment areas because these are where the students and the parents look for an explanation of the grade. This is where parents can find the information on what the student needs to improve upon. If the student learns quickly, say so. Even good students need encouragement, and most of them will have your comments and praise reinforced by their parents.

A good way to look at planning lessons and creating assessments is to remember they are the means to help your students achieve good grades. These are important tasks that you must complete, in addition to grading homework, but homework can also be a workload that you may want to consider before assigning.

That Nasty Little Word — Homework

Remember, you have to grade whatever you assign. This does not mean you should not teach as you normally would, but that you should attempt to keep large assignments, or in-depth assignments, spaced out. It will make life easier for you and keep your stress level at a minimum.

Part of any lesson plan should include the homework you will assign. You do not want to assign homework just to give students busy work. Your homework assignments should be a reinforcement of the material you are teaching. Homework should also be a way for students to show signs they are learning the information you have been relaying.

Preparing your students for homework assignments

Your job as a teacher is to let the students and the parents know at the beginning of the school year exactly what your expectations are when it comes to homework assignments. It is also a good idea to give parents a paper with this information, as well as tips to help their children accomplish good homework habits. Some of those tips might include:

- A quiet place to study
- Good lighting in their study area
- Plenty of school supplies
- Establishing a homework routine

Be sure to give the parents a list of the supplies the children will need for homework, such as crayons, construction paper, scissors, glue, paper, and anything else you feel they will need. Giving this information to the parents and students at the beginning of the year will help eliminate problems in the future, and you will find that parents are grateful for your input.

Is homework necessary?

There are experts who argue homework is not necessary for students to do well in school. They say that because students and parents are so busy with sports, organizations, jobs, and other involvements, homework is too much added stress. These experts also say if homework is not eliminated, it should at least be seriously reduced. There is indeed such a thing as too much homework, and too much will have the opposite effect of what you are trying to achieve.

So how much homework is too much? The following story is a prime example of too much homework.

There was a teacher who gave her students at least 50 minutes of homework nightly. Many nights, the homework load was as much as two and a half hours. The parents complained to one another, but no one felt comfortable enough to speak with the teacher. It was more than two months before one of the parents approached the teacher with her concern, but to no avail. When word of this was passed through the chain of parents, this only verified their feelings that the teacher was unapproachable. The parent then took the complaint to the next level in the chain of command. Again, this did no good, so the parent continued to move up the ladder with her complaints. Being an involved parent, she had saved the child's homework papers that were brought home and took the student's homework folder to the assistant superintendent.

The child's homework folder was more than 6 inches thick, and this was only three months into the school year. The student was in was the fourth grade. Another important fact was the student was an A+ student. If an A+ student was struggling with the amount of homework given, how hard must it have been for the students who were average, or less than average and had a difficult time with learning?

The teacher attended a private meeting with administrators, and they explained an important factor that she had either never learned or forgotten: Listen to your students and their parents. While this may be inconvenient at times, and time may be short, it is an important part of being an effective teacher.

There are several objectives to learn from this story. One of the most important is to be approachable and flexible. If a parent comes to you with concerns, it is your job as a teacher to hear those concerns and take them into serious consideration. *This will be discussed more in Chapter 9.* Another lesson to be learned is that the amount of homework you give should not be so taxing that the students are overwhelmed to the point of being unable to learn.

As an elementary teacher, you are in total control of how much homework a student has. You are in control of all assignments and the amount of time these assignments take. You should always consider areas where your students need more learning time, but you must also consider your class as a whole. Although you may have a number of excellent students, you will most likely also have students who are below average or students with disabilities. While it may take an excellent student 30 minutes to do their homework assignment, it may take the others more than two hours.

Another consideration when it comes to too much homework: When students spend seven hours in school and two to three hours being with family — which includes parents, friends, meals, and chores — how much time does that leave them? So far, they have put in a ten-hour day, and if they get any time for sleep and relaxation, that is another eight to ten hours, which adds up to be an 18- to 20-hour day. That leaves a maximum of four to six hours for homework. Is it really good for young children to have their day so completely filled? This is a time for physical growth as well as mental, and that alone takes a toll on young children.

You should check your school's policy on homework before giving assignments. Some school districts have implemented a policy that homework should never exceed ten minutes per grade. This would mean ten minutes for first grade, 20 minutes for second grade, and so on. This gives time for reinforcement for the day's learning and still leaves enough hours in the day for the children to have much needed family time and free time.

Some tips for assigning homework

The best time to assign homework is when you are closing the lesson for the subject you are teaching. Writing the homework assignments on the board and having the students write the assignment in their homework folder in the morning is a good habit to develop. It is also a good idea to give a brief reminder of homework assignments at the end of the day. Keep in mind that if you give three assignments at the end of the day, by that time the students are tired and may resent the assignments. By giving the homework mission in the morning and at the closing of the subject, it does not seem so daunting.

Another good practice is having students routinely turn in their homework. With younger students, you may have them get into the practice of putting away their backpack after getting out the homework folder, putting their homework folder into a collection area, and then getting their desk or table area ready for the day. With the older students, you might have a student gather the homework assignments while you take attendance or make last-minute adjustments to the daily lesson plan.

There is also the problem of students who do not do their homework. How do you handle this, and what should the consequences be? As a teacher of young students, the first thing to do is inform the parents. Then you must deal with the student and the consequences. You should pull the student aside, ask why the homework was not turned in, and then decide what the consequences should be, if any. There are times when homework assignments are not done due to money issues. Believe it or not, there have been teachers who have had students not turn in homework simply because the family could not afford to buy paper. If you suspect a case such as this, it would be wise to discreetly slip a few pieces of blank paper inside the homework folder. This is a way to ensure the student does not miss out on the reinforcement of the daily lesson and also a way to avoid embarrassing the student or the family.

If the reason the student is not doing homework is simply because he or she does not want to, it will be up to you to decide on the consequences. It is possible you could have the student or students do their homework in the hallway during class. You could have them miss a portion of recess to do their homework at that time. Perhaps they could skip library visit day and stay in the classroom with you to do homework instead. Just be careful how you approach and correct the issue because some parents feel some consequences are too harsh for elementary students.

Homework is the link between home and school, and parents are your most important ally in having the students accomplish this task. This is a two-way street; your students' parents should always feel comfortable in approaching you about any subject, including homework. You should also always keep the parents informed because this kind of cooperation keeps all parties happy, and the child will be successful in learning.

With the classroom prepared for the beginning of the year, it is time to get ready for the demands of the job, and knowing what to expect is half the battle.

Chapter 5

Prepare for the Demands of the Job

Paperwork by the Pound

As we have already established, teaching students is merely a small portion of your job. There is paperwork that you will have to deal with on a daily basis, and there is paperwork that you will have to attend to periodically.

First, we will look at the daily paperwork that will demand your attention. If the paperwork is not given your attention on a daily basis, it will multiply, and your desk will disappear underneath it.

Recording grades and keeping attendance

According to veteran teachers, the two biggest record-keeping responsibilities you have as a teacher are keeping attendance and recording grades. You may think recording grades is more important than keeping attendance, but they are equally important. Your attendance records are legal documents and, if necessary, these records can be subpoenaed into court. The attendance records can also be subpoenaed for criminal cases or custody battles, which does happen. Recording or not recording a child's attendance can change lives. The best way to ensure you carry out this responsibility on a regular basis is to make it part of your daily routine.

It would be wise to use a good grade book in which you can record not only grades, but also attendance. You can make your own system or even make your own grade book to do this. You can use symbols or numbers to record attendance, but if you do this, be sure to write each symbol or number and what it means in the front part of your grade book. This way, if your records are ever subpoenaed or your recordkeeping is checked by your administrators, it will make sense.

Once the grades and attendance are recorded in your grade book, be sure to follow up by recording the same data on your computer. It is a good idea to have two forms of records, so if one of them were ever missing (say, if your computer crashed or you lost your grade book), you still have one set of records. It only takes a few minutes, and if you do this on a daily basis, perhaps at the end of each day, it will make your life much easier in the long run.

Parents' notes

After grades and attendance, the most important papers to keep track of are parents' notes in regard to the student's way of getting home, medications, or emergency information. Doctors' orders fall under the same level of significance. These papers need to be filed, and some will need to be turned in to the office. For the ones turned in to the office, you may want to make a copy before doing so.

Lesson plans and assessments

You are also going to want to make copies of your lesson plans, quizzes, tests, or methods of evaluation. These will come in handy for many years, and you will be glad you filed them for future reference. Having extra copies of these will also come in handy should you have to miss work one day and need a substitute to fill in for you. *More about this will be explained later in this chapter.*

When making copies for class assignments, there are ways to avoid those frustrating days of waiting for the copier or wishing you had used that broken down machine the day before when it was still working. Many schools are on a tight budget, and copies are sometimes limited. This can cause headaches if you are not prepared; it would be wise to ask the secretary or another teacher what the rules are about making copies. Some schools do not allow teachers to touch the copy machine, and it is best if you know this before school starts. There is also the familiar scenario of teachers waiting in line to use the copier while the class is wreaking havoc down the hallway. These are reasons to plan ahead and make sure you take care of any copies you may need for a lesson.

You have already recorded the attendance and grades; you have that paperwork out of the way; and messages from parents and doctors have been taken care of. Now it is time to rid your desk of some more papers as quickly as possible.

Filing paperwork

Pay particular attention to your secretary's notes regarding phone calls. These are extremely important, especially if the calls are from administration or parents, because these are people you do not want to ignore no matter how tired you are. Remember, you want the parents to know you are approachable, and you care about their child. It is also in your best interest to return calls from administration promptly.

All of the paperwork you have to keep track of will be one of the most stressful parts of your job, which is why it is so dire to plan ahead and stay abreast of paperwork as it comes in. According to Julia G. Thompson, veteran teacher of more than 25 years, the average teacher will have to handle more than 10,000 student papers, and this is in just one school year. Thompson recommends you have three choices when it comes to the paperwork that finds your desk or mailbox: act on it, file it away, or throw it in the trash. Obviously, you may not be able to act on all paperwork as it comes in, but what you cannot attend to immediately, you can take care of during the 30 minutes you arrive early, the 30 minutes you stay after school, or that allotted work time you have slotted into the evening when you get home.

There are categories of paperwork that you will want to keep separated. These categories are:

- Attendance to be recorded

- Papers to be graded
- Papers to be entered into the grade book
- Papers to go to the office
- Papers to be copied
- Handouts to go home
- Late work and make-up assignments
- Emergency information
- Notes from parents

If you look over that list again, you will notice that another form of paperwork that can stack up quickly is late work or make-up assignments. These can set you back and force you to fall behind rather quickly, so as soon as they come in, mark them in your record book and on your computer. Sometimes teachers can become frustrated or angry with a student because these late papers can cause headaches. Remind yourself that this is just a part of the job, and you chose this career; the student did not choose it for you.

Preparing For a Substitute

One more area of paperwork that needs to be brought to your attention is preparation for a substitute teacher and the assignments, grades, and recording that will come with it. Lack of preparation for your substitute can cause a major headache for the substitute and give the class absence of routine and time on their hands, which can create havoc. As a teacher, it is your responsibility to make sure you have lesson plans for a substitute.

To be well-prepared for a substitute to walk into your classroom and take over where you have left off, it is advisable to have an emergency set of lesson plans in a folder available at all times. These plans can be generic, such as a paper of addition or multiplication problems students can do in class or pictures to color, but there should be copies of papers the class will have to do. The copies should already be made so the substitute does not have to make them while the class is left to destroy the room.

You can find generic material for your class that will reinforce whatever they have learned or will be learning. You can have math problems for them to solve, or you can have the students read aloud. You may also want to add a list of sponge activities for the substitute. Sponge activities are fillers that take up extra time the substitute might find on his or her hands. These kinds of activities do not have to be related to your academic studies, but they are important to have available. Here are a few ideas for sponge activities:

- Take a word such as "multimedia" and have students create as many words as they can from the letters

- Count by fives or tens to 100 or more, depending on age group

- Have each student add a line to a story that you begin

- Create a mural

- Finger paint, color, or draw a picture of a favorite family activity

- Practice or make flash cards

- Have a spelling bee

Teachers are advised to have two folders ready for their substitute teachers. Your first folder should contain the general academic assignments for the students to work on. The second folder should hold general information on your students, containing the following:

- A seating chart and class roster including students' special needs or problems

- Your discipline system

- Fire drill procedures and a map of where your class is to be taken

- A map of the school and grounds, especially for extra duties as playground or cafeteria duty

- Names of staff members the substitute may need to work with

- Substitute checklist of schedule and times allotted for various classroom activities

- Substitute feedback form for necessary information

- Your home or cell phone number in case you are needed

- Names of students who are pulled out of class for various reasons

- The roster of students marked with how they are to go home

The preparation of the substitute folders is very time-consuming. It is highly advisable to have these folders complete and ready to go before the first day of school even begins. You may need to update this folder as the school year progresses, but having this responsibility taken care of and out of the way will be a huge burden off your shoulders. In the long run, you and your substitute will appreciate your preparation, and your students' learning time and routine will not be disrupted.

After looking at some of the responsibilities, possibilities, and probabilities involving the paperwork you will have to deal with, once again it is easy to see why being prepared and committed to your job is so important for you and your students.

Solutions For Technology Problems

For some teachers, technology is the liberator of education; for others, it is a nightmare. For the schools in which the students are from the project areas, technology is the nightmare of education, not only for the teachers, but also the students. More often than not, funds for technology are not available in these areas. Then there are the schools where money is readily available for technology. The technological inconsistency between the different schools is so vast, it is almost unbelievable.

There are schools that have not only funds for computer labs, but also one or more computers per classroom and high-speed Internet. There are also schools that cannot get enough funding to purchase more than one computer for a classroom. Then there are the schools that manage to gather enough funds to have a few computers in a specified room, such as the library, but there are not enough computers there to meet the needs of the teachers and students.

If you give an assignment that requires Internet access, perhaps having your students look up information on the woolly mammoth for science class, you should explain to the class that the time frame for the assignment will be adjusted for those who do not have a computer or Internet access at home. You should also explain they may find a friend who may have Internet, be given extra time in class to use the school computer, or take advantage of using the local public library's computer where Internet is available. Another option is to have an alternative assignment for the students who do not have a computer or access to the Internet, perhaps allowing students to use books for information rather than the Internet. As a teacher, be aware that some students do not have access to a computer or the Internet. It can be upsetting for parents to experience their children's worry and frustration due to such an oversight.

Teaching and technology

Some teachers are fortunate enough to have computer labs but avoid them at all costs because they see computers as an annoyance. Sometimes this is due to the teacher's being unfamiliar with computers, but some people just do not like new technology.

The first rule of using technology in teaching is for the teacher to become proficient in using the tools. There is nothing more frustrating, for both you and your students, than a teacher trying to learn a program when he or she is supposed to be teaching. If your district offers any training, make sure you take advantage of this opportunity. When dealing with computer programs and digital cameras, some training is especially useful. When you learn how to use these programs, you will be able to use them in your lessons.

Be aware that many students are growing up in an environment that is filled with technology. For some students this has led to a much shorter attention span, and this has also led them to expect to be entertained. Multimedia allows students to be creative in various ways. This is a plus for students who are normally not active learners because you can use several concepts involving technology to improve your lessons and help your students learn more effectively. Of course, this is if your school district has the technology for you to use.

Students usually love to use new technology because they find it to be fun and entertaining. Working with young people who are excited about learning is entertaining and encouraging for you as a teacher. To see children's eyes light up when you walk into the classroom with a tool of technology is gratifying. When your students are excited about learning, you know you are on the right track.

Problems with implementing technology

Integrating technology into lesson plans can be difficult because of the lack of time available to teachers. Sometimes teachers need to find the time to learn something new, and on top of that, they have to find the time to figure out how to integrate the technology into their lesson plans. It seems administrators sometimes forget that by the time teachers have met all their previous demands, they are too tired and drained to create ways in which to add the technology into lessons that have already been created.

This lack of vision when it comes to implementing technology or software is a problem on the administrative side. Many times technology is purchased and implemented into the schools and is not even useful. If an administrator buys a software package without realizing the certification allows it to be loaded on only one computer, there is a problem. Which teacher gets the software? There are times when software will be purchased and it is discovered teachers cannot use the software because they do not understand it.

If you are a teacher in a school that does not have funding for technology, you may be able to apply for a technology grant. Be aware that grant writing is not an easy task, so you will want to do some research before applying. If you are lucky enough to receive a grant, remember that some grants have stipulations that you must keep a record of how your students are progressing toward the goal you stated in your application.

Budget Cuts + Out-of-Pocket Expenses = Getting Creative

Go to any online search engine and type in "school budget cuts" and you will see just how badly the spiral of the economy in the United States is hurting school funding. Out-of-pocket expenses have been a problem for teachers for a long time, but the problem has become so intense lately that many states have entitled teachers to a tax deduction or tax credit for purchasing classroom supplies. This ongoing problem is getting worse, and teachers are forced to find a way to deal with it.

There is actually more money available for teaching supplies than what you might realize. The first place to look is your principal, because some of school districts allocate a certain amount of money per teacher for supplies. The next place to check is your school's Parent Teacher Association (PTA) or PTO. Many PTAs and PTOs are more than happy to help the teachers with money if they have it. More often than not, if they do not have the money, they will hold fundraisers to raise the funds. State lottery money is supposed to go to education, and it is fine for you to ask your administrator if any of that money goes to the teachers for supplies. According to the California Department of Education, during fiscal year 2007-2008, the lottery generated $1.1 billion for education. It looks and sounds like a lot of money, but broken down, it is only $132.20 per student. The California lottery is only 1.5 percent of all education funding, which is not much when you consider the money supported 8.329 million students. It is not wise to expect a lot of lottery money to fund teacher supplies because there are not a lot of funds to go around.

While speaking with your principal about money for supplies, you should also ask about how the items in the supply room are to be accessed. Some schools have an open-door policy where teachers may enter and take what they need, but unfortunately, this open-door policy is becoming obsolete. Now, many schools are keeping the supply room door closed; teachers must sign for any supplies taken; and there is usually a limit on what you can take and how much. If you are in a school where you must sign for supplies, be sure to think before you order. The cut-off point comes faster than what you might realize and, from that point on, you are going to have to purchase the rest of the supplies on your own. School districts will also take orders for supplies, allotting a certain amount of money and allowing you to order from a supply list. There is usually someone in charge of the ordering, such as a secretary or custodian, and that would be the person to speak with on how much you are allowed to spend and when they will be taking supply orders.

With budget cuts getting deeper, it has become more common and necessary for teachers to revert to finding their own materials for activities. Veteran teachers all over the country can attest that budget cuts and out-of-pocket expenses are through the roof.

CASE STUDY: TIPS FROM VETERAN TEACHERS

Tina Caldarelli, Second-grade and
emotional support teacher
Cheston Elementary
Easton, Pennsylvania

Merrisa Herman, First-grade teacher
Shumaker Elementary
Bellevue, Ohio

Merrisa Herman said she is guilty of spending money each year on her classroom but adds that the expenses get smaller with each passing year. "I ask the parents for a lot of donations. Some are more than willing to help," she said. Parents are also happy to help and generally will do so when asked. If you use common household objects such as plastic bottles, milk jugs, paper plates, clothespins, buttons, yarn, and other everyday objects, you will surely have their cooperation.

Tina Caldarelli suggests teachers "order only what you need. Share materials with other teachers. You would be surprised what other teachers have stashed in their cabinets and closets. Also, utilize the library instead of buying your own books for a specific lesson." Caldarelli admits that it is "difficult not to spend money," when it comes to out-of-pocket expenses. She advises teachers to "use coupons, look for sales, and shop at the dollar stores. After the first few years, you begin to accumulate materials. Make sure you laminate all posters and try to keep what you buy in good condition."

Because certain materials are harder to come by than others, you may find it necessary to alter some of your planned activities. It will be helpful for you to look over your lesson plans and activities to make a list of the supplies you will need for each activity. Also, while you are making your supply list for each activity, write the date for when the activity is scheduled to take place beside it. Once you have finished your dated list of supplies, you have a decision to make: You can consider the supplies you will need for the first six or eight weeks and begin looking for them before school starts, or you can send letters to the parents of your students and ask if they could start saving or looking for certain materials you will be using.

If you decide to gather the first six or eight weeks of materials yourself, you can plan to send a letter home with students on the first day of school, asking the parents to save things for future activities. It is a good idea to give parents a list during Open House when you can speak with them about the need for help. Be honest with them because they will appreciate your honesty and be more willing to help. Parents do realize that by helping you with materials, they are helping their child.

Between the PTO or the PTA, the supply room, and your allotted money from the district, it will be a start on what you will need. There are other places to look to find materials that you may need, such as:

- Garage sales
- Craft and sewing stores
- Local newspapers
- Local industries
- Printing stores
- Grocery stores
- Thrift shops

Let your imagination run wild when you go to these places, always keeping in mind the possibilities of creative activities. Do you think your students would enjoy putting on a play? Thrift stores are full of clothes of all styles, hats, shoes, and many other items that could be used. Go to a store that sells material and items for sewing. There are bags of buttons, balls of yarn, spools of thread, and many more treasures to be found. Local newspapers are usually willing to give away the ends of paper rolls because they are useless for printing. This paper is great for finger painting or creating murals for history lessons. Grocery stores and local industries will be thankful to have you pick up empty boxes rather than pay someone to take them away.

If you are somewhat lacking in creativity, do not worry. There are plenty of ideas for activities floating around on the Internet and in books, and many of these ideas give a list of materials you will need with directions. Games are another way to be creative with your students because kids love learning and playing new games. Again, you can find thousands of unique games online and in books. *Some places to find these ideas will be listed in this book under Resources.*

Making your budget stretch

School supplies and field trips are the places most schools look to cut when budgets are tight, so putting your creative streak to work is now crucial for all teachers. Be sure to share ideas and any extra supplies you may have. Your colleagues will appreciate this, and they will be more likely to do the same.

Some handy household items students can bring from home and their uses are:

- Jars to hold pencils or pens

- Boxes can hold papers or large projects

- Cans of all sizes can be decorated and used for holding paper clips, pencils, or flowers

- Plastic plant containers can be used for decorating Mother's Day gifts

- Plain coffee cups can be decorated for Father's Day. Because Mother's Day falls during the school year, many schools use the celebration of Father's Day for art projects before school is dismissed for summer

You should not feel badly about asking parents for their help, and another good way to keep them informed is to consider a newsletter. You will be surprised how many of them will go on a search, asking their work colleagues, neighbors, or family members for supplies they are willing to donate. Do not forget that parents are your partners when it comes to their kids.

The impact of budget cuts

The many ways budget cuts affect teachers is surprising, and most of these effects are in areas people do not think to even consider. In a profession where approximately 20 percent of teachers leave within the first three years, budget cuts will just give these teachers more reason to give up on their chosen field. We will look at a list of some of the ways budget cuts will affect teachers and discuss each item:

- Less pay
- Fewer supplies
- Limited access to technology and software
- Decreased teacher benefits
- Outdated textbooks
- Eliminating elective courses
- Eliminating professional development opportunities
- School closures
- Forced moves
- Overcrowded classrooms

Less pay: Teachers will probably give up any raises for years to come, and the ones who take on extra duties for pay will see that go out the window immediately. Most of the schools have already cut summer school and sports or other activities — all areas where teachers could earn more pay.

Fewer supplies: As we have already stated, materials and supplies are usually the first cuts to be made, and these are necessary items that teachers were already digging into their pockets to provide for their students.

Technology and software: If your school was limited on technology and or software in the past few years, they will not be getting any now. Teachers who may have ordered, or were planning to order, new software for enhancing lessons will be disappointed when the programs are unobtainable due to lack of funds. Unfortunately, the ones who will pay the steepest price are the students.

Decreased teacher benefits: With the budget cuts going as deep as they are today, many teachers may experience both salary cuts and cuts in medical benefits.

Outdated textbooks: It is unbelievable how many schools have textbooks that are outdated; some of the material is so old it is now known to be incorrect. Scientists make new discoveries every day, proving that some old theories were incorrect. With the financial problems the schools are now facing, there is a good chance it will often be a very long time before new textbooks are seen.

Eliminating elective courses: These courses are what makes some students more fortunate than others, but said courses are about to become a thing of the past. If the cuts are too deep, elective courses will be eliminated, and teaching jobs will go out the door with them. Not only will it force teachers into teaching courses they are not ready to teach, but it will also decrease students' knowledge, options, and opportunities.

Eliminating professional development opportunities: Most communities regard this effect with a "So what?" attitude. What these communities do not realize is that theories, teaching methods, students, improvements for students with special needs, and geographic ethnicities change each year. Without these professional development opportunities, teachers will fall behind in what is an integral part of the students' ever-changing education.

School closures: Everyone knows that smaller schools are better for students and teachers, but when budget cuts get too deep, smaller schools are forced to close, and students are relocated to larger schools. Even veteran teachers who worked in smaller schools and were teaching the subjects and grades they loved most are forced to teach whatever is available. This is not good for the students or the teachers.

Forced moves: Even if a school is not forced to close its doors, they may be forced to increase class sizes or reduce the courses offered. This will force teachers with less seniority to move to a new area, so they may find another teaching job.

Overcrowded classrooms: Overcrowded classrooms create more demands on a teacher and take away individual attention and care. A larger class means more disruptions and more stress on students and teachers alike. It has been proved time and again that smaller classes are better for the students and for the teachers.

How budget cuts and the economy may affect your students

It is amazing how budget cuts being made elsewhere can affect teachers and their students. For example, the recent 31 percent budget cut for public libraries in Ohio will force many of the public libraries to close or run part-time, and as we have already determined, that is the only source of computer and Internet for some students. Cuts have been made in funding for the arts across the nation, and some community centers and art communities will shut down. These are places many children are involved in, leaving them nowhere to find these resources for activities. If students were heavily involved in plays at the local art center, they will miss that part of their life, and it may show in their grades.

With the downfall of the economy and job losses so high, many families are being forced to move, sometimes more than once, which will create a high fluctuation in the number of students changing schools. Teachers will see students come and go, and students will feel the loss of their friends moving away. All this affects kids and how they perform in their academic studies. Many people do not realize the effect budget cuts have, and will have, on teachers and their students, and what the short- and long-term consequences might be.

As an effective teacher, it will be up to you to pay close attention to such happenings, changes in your students, and the possible consequences that could come with these changes. If you see a student going down the wrong road, perhaps stealing from other students, will you be able to intervene and help him or her find the right path back? Students have always needed effective teachers, and now they will need them more than ever. More budget cuts are inevitable, meaning there will be more demands on teachers to help their students maintain a good attitude, and effective teachers will have more to watch for in concern for their students' well-being.

Now that you have a better idea of what to expect from the demands of your job, it is a good idea to consider ways to make your job easier to handle.

Chapter 6
Tips to Make Your Job Easier

Making the Best of Overcrowded Classrooms

Overcrowding in schools is a nationwide epidemic that leads to more problems such as discipline issues. More students are harder to control, and one discipline problem with 40 students in the room can quickly escalate into more than what it started out to be. Trying to get a few students under control is hard enough, but once 40 students are out of control, it can be almost impossible to get them calmed down and back on their assignment.

Some tips on managing an overcrowded classroom are:

- Be a positive thinker and students will follow your lead.

- Make a good connection with your students. If you have a good connection with your students, it will not matter if there are 20 or 40 students in your classroom.

- Be prepared and committed to your vocation and whatever else needs to happen for the welfare of you and your students.

- Keep your lessons interesting, captivating your students and encouraging them to interact with the lessons, and this will help maintain a cooperative, enjoyable learning environment.

- Enlist the help of your students, allowing them to run slight errands such as taking absenteeism slips to the office, eliminating some of your stress.

- Create a team environment.

- Stick with class routine.

- Teach common courtesy by using it.

- Keep the noise level at a minimum because loud noise only makes kids want to be louder.

- Pay attention to room arrangement, making it as open and user-friendly as possible.

- Stay on top of the grading of papers to reduce your stress.

- Greet your students individually with a smile each morning; it will help them and you keep a positive attitude.

Students' ability to focus is another problem that comes with overcrowding, especially if there are one or more students who create distractions. New teachers especially find overcrowding frustrating because they are in a learning period of their career. Truth be told, even veteran teachers cannot meet the needs of every child in an overcrowded classroom. This does not mean teachers should not, or do not, try; it simply means it is close to impossible to do.

Asking for help is imperative when you have an overloaded class. Ask parents to come in as volunteers, especially if there is no possibility of getting a teacher's aide. Peer tutoring can help lighten your load, and it is good for the students to have their colleagues help them when you cannot. Another idea to lighten your load is using the buddy system. Pairing students can be helpful to you and to them, but it is advisable to do this after you have gotten to know the students better.

Classroom shortages

One of the ways some school districts choose to cope with overcrowding is by utilizing mobile classrooms, also known as portable classrooms. Mobile classroom units are a common sight around the schools today.

Floating teachers (teachers who do not have a room but must move from one temporarily available room to another) are also common due to over-crowding. When a room is not being used during a certain time frame, a floating teacher is assigned to use that room for his or her class. Being a floating teacher is one of the most frustrating situations for a new teacher to find himself or herself in because it produces some annoying situations and challenges. Floating can cause problems with other teachers who feel their room is their space; even if they realize that you do not want to walk through that doorway as a floating teacher, they may resent your presence. A teacher who has had a room to himself or herself for years and finds he or she now has to share the space may feel his or her territory is being invaded. Just try to remember not to take the attitude personally, and be sure to leave each room as you found it. Be thoughtful, but do not allow these teachers to treat you poorly. The advantage to being a floating teacher is if you rise to the occasion and the challenges, you will likely become a fantastic teacher.

Not enough textbooks to go around

You may find you do not have enough textbooks, which is a common dilemma in many schools. This can cause problems for assigning readings from the book. When there are not enough textbooks to go around, the books most likely stay in the classroom. Some schools have what is known as class sets of textbooks, which means the books must be accounted for in the classroom at all times. A good way to keep track of the books is to have students sign for them any time they are taken from the classroom for homework. Even with a tracking method in place, you will find that books still come up missing. When this is what you are facing, you may want to make copies of the questions for your students or copy sections of the book for homework reading. One way around this is to do all the readings in class, but keep in mind that it makes homework harder because students are answering questions by memory alone.

Believe it or not, some teachers are forced to teach with no textbooks at all. It is advisable to talk to veteran teachers about this problem. Most likely they will have good advice to share and help you find solutions.

Too many bodies, not enough seats

A shortage of desks for students can become a problem with overcrowded classrooms; this is where the earlier suggestion of having an extra desk or two available will come in handy. If you find there is a shortage, remember it is most likely a temporary situation that may last only a week or two. Not only is it possible that some students will move out of the area, but they may be moved to a different class, or another teacher may have too many desks in his or her room due to a small class. Do not wait until two weeks pass to report the lack of desk space to your administrator, but realize it may take a while to get what you need. If you must set up temporary accommodations, a table and chairs will suffice for a while.

Overcrowding in the news

Overcrowding is a stressful issue for teachers and administrators alike. The problems that arise due to overcrowding can become major obstacles. According to teachers surveyed for a report by the National Economics and Social Rights Initiative organization, there is a small increase in school violence with overcrowding because students are harder to control. The National School Safety Center reports that school safety statistics show that issues involving overcrowding, fighting/violence/gangs, and drugs remain in the top five identified most pressing educational problems. According to a report by the Association for Supervision and Curriculum Development — an organization that develops services for educators — overcrowded classrooms hamper educator's efforts to know their students, and the results are often misunderstandings, frustrations, and violence.

In 2008, the National Economic and Social Rights Initiative (NESRI) and Teachers Unite published a report based on surveys from more than 300 middle and high school teachers in 130 New York City public schools, focus groups, and interviews with over a dozen teachers. This gathering of information revealed the following:

- Seven percent of teachers feel that overcrowding and large class sizes are the largest threat to safety.

- City and state policymakers allow overcrowding and deny needed resources.

- Overcrowding is one of the main barriers in creating positive school experiences.

Schools in Santa Ana, California, were penalized and took a loss of $2 million in state funding for failing to keep elementary classes limited and because administrators asked teachers to sign fake lists of students, better known as rosters. In July 2007, the school administrators did not add the special education students who were taught in regular classrooms to the student roster so it would appear state restrictions on the number of students allowed in a classroom were being met. By meeting the allowances, the schools would receive funding that is known as class size-reduction funding. With the misleading numbers given by administrators, the schools received $549,696 in state funding. This incorrect information was eventually discovered, the school funding was cut, and the money was returned.

The problem of overcrowded classrooms is not limited to big cities, as many people believe. The problem persists in suburban and rural school districts as well, and sometimes the overcrowding in rural and suburban schools is even worse than in the big cities. The fact is there are too few classrooms to adequately house and educate all the students in the country.

Students and teachers sometimes find themselves forced into cramped spaces that were never meant to be classrooms because of overcrowding. Cramped areas plus too many bodies equals health problems. Overcrowding causes more than just the adverse effect on learning; the spread of colds, influenza, skin disorders, and other health issues are more widespread in classrooms that have a large number of students.

Research as far back as 1988 has proved that congested classrooms cause more stress for teachers and it also leads to more teacher absenteeism due to physical sickness and stress. This also means the teacher is more likely to catch whatever germ happens to be floating around on any given day. Not only are common viruses a normal concern for teachers, but now teachers must be conscious of the problems arising from swine flu. The H1N1 virus hit the United States over the summer of 2009, causing more than 80 outbreaks in more than 40 states. The Centers for Disease Control and Prevention reported that as of November 12, 2009, there were more than 4,000 deaths caused by swine flu or complications due to swine flu in the United States alone.

In 2008, enrollment figures showed some schools in New York were as much as 200 percent over capacity. Many teachers agree overcrowding affects their instructional techniques. In May 2009, the Campaign for Fiscal Equity reported that overcrowding is one of the causes for low academic performance. The Campaign for Fiscal Equity is calling for New York City's leaders to develop a strategy to combat the problem of overcrowding in the local schools. In September 2009, the NYC Public School Parents, a Web site written by and for parents of students in New York public schools, reported that there were "1,600 fewer classroom teachers and 10,000 more out-of-classroom staff." However, the New York Department of Education insists "the size of teaching corps is in line with the student population."

Early burnout is another effect stuffed classrooms have on teachers, and it is an important point to consider. According to a survey taken in 2008, 76 percent of first year teachers said that having fewer students in a classroom would be a very effective way of improving teacher quality. Teachers and students alike feel overwhelmed, discouraged, and disgusted with the space shortage and its consequences for learning. Students complained their papers were not checked daily, and they did not feel comfortable taking part in class discussions or special projects. The report also stated that teachers are deeply disturbed by overcrowding and staff stress management related to the problem. Teachers have also reported overcrowding as the largest threat to safety due to tension and chaos created by sharing a crowded space. The exasperation and frustration teachers experience because of the inability to have good relationships with their students in overcrowded classrooms was another major concern, according to a report made by the National Economic and Social Rights Initiative and Teachers Unite organization.

Though overcrowding is a major concern, it is still possible to survive teaching under these conditions. Holding your students' attention is a priority, but once you have that attention, you are building a team environment. Remember the tips given in this chapter for surviving overcrowded classrooms and it will help to relieve the stress.

But yet another stress factor is memorizing names, especially if you have a classroom filled with a large number of students.

Tricks for Memorizing Names

It may not seem like much to teachers, but incorrectly pronouncing or spelling a student's name can cause resentment. Being able to call your students by name is the first step in getting to know them, creating a relationship with them, and gaining their respect, which helps you maintain control of your classroom.

One way to begin this process of learning your students' names and their proper spellings is to review their records. While you look over the folder of each student, write their first and last name, then jot down notes beside each of them. This will help you remember specifics for each student and therefore help you remember their names.

The following are some tips for helping you to remember your students' names:

- Make a seating chart, study the class roster, and create name tags for your students.

- Have students sit in assigned seats so you may associate names with faces for a few weeks.

- When you read forms from your students, mentally picture their face with the information you are reading.

- Walk around the room while students are working, checking the roll with each pupil.

- On the first day of school, have each student say his or her name and repeat it.

- Note pronunciation remarks on your roster and mark notes about characteristics for each student.

- If you forget a child's name, admit it and ask for help. When the child says his or her name, repeat it, write it down, and say it again.

Helping your students get to know one another is another way to learn about your students and also helps them learn to value one each other. Some ideas to help students learn about one another while you learn about them are:

- Take attendance out loud and have students raise their hand when their name is called.

- Put name tags on the desk tops, being careful to spell them correctly.

- Have the students wear a name tag the first two or three days of school.

- Pass out papers as you walk around the room. Call out the student's name, have them raise their hand, then take their paper to them.

- Pass around a large calendar and have each student mark their name and birthday appropriately. Hang the calendar on the wall for the school year.

- Pass around a map and have students mark the city where they were born.

- Have students tell something about themselves or their family that they would like to share.

- Take pictures of your students, and have the students bring in a picture from when they were younger. Post those photos beside the pictures you have taken.

- Have your students keep a daily journal, allowing them to write whatever they wish. Teachers have been doing this for many years, and it has become a common way to help students learn spelling and writing. It is also therapeutic. You will learn a variety of things about your students and their families from this assignment, but express to the students that it should be about family, their pets, or maybe a favorite television show. Your directions on what to write in their journal will be based on their grade level, but most teachers in upper elementary grades do not use the journal method due to parents' feeling it is an invasion of family privacy.

If you have a large number of students, it may be difficult to immediately memorize your students' names. If it is too hard to learn all their names right away, learn only a few and use them during that first day. On the second day, learn a few more, and so on until you have learned all of them.

There will be times when you might forget a student's name, especially if the child is quiet. It is also hard to remember who is whom if students with similar names sit together. Just remember that repetition is a proven way to move information from short-term memory to long-term memory. When you forget a student's name, it makes them feel humiliated and unimportant, so be sure to work on this right away.

Surviving the Daily Grind

Every day of each school year, you are going to be faced with a list of things that must be accomplished. Your first priority will be to record attendance and have meaningful and engaging lessons for your class. Your second priority is to grade the lesson assignments, meet with any students who ask to speak with you, make parent and administrative phone calls, meet with any administrators if necessary, and meet with any extracurricular groups you are involved with. Recording grades and dealing with the paperwork should be done before you leave the school in hopes of clearing your desk before starting a new day.

Life can sometimes be hard and demanding, and being a teacher will likely add to your stress. As a teacher, you will most likely feel as though your work is never done, which is a horrible feeling that may make it difficult for you to relax. When your day is over, you should be able to go home and feel free, enjoying your evening or your weekend with your family or pet. There are three things that help you accomplish this, and they are:

- Setting goals
- Prioritizing
- Organizing

Setting goals

Creating your goals will help you see where you have been and where you want to go. This will help you start the beginning of the school year successfully. Most schools have mid-term progress reports, and a week or two before these are due is a good time to take a few minutes to once again see where you have been and set new goals. Not only will this help you balance your time at school, but also at home so that you may enjoy your free time.

If you set long-term and short-term goals and analyze your progress periodically, it will help you keep up with what is working for you and your students and what is not. This is a good way to keep a tight grip on your priorities.

Prioritizing

Setting your priorities will help you eliminate stress. Most effective teachers are at work approximately half an hour to an hour before the students begin to arrive, and they typically stay a half-hour to an hour after the students leave. Staying after school gives teachers time to grade papers; speak with parents, students, or administrators; and make phone calls. This extra time at school eliminates having to take work home, which should be a major priority. By prioritizing your daily tasks, you will manage your time more effectively, ridding the possibility of burnout and stress.

There will be times you will not have that extra time before and after school due to staff meetings, professional development meetings, seminars, and committee meetings. By being as consistent as possible with this extra time twice a day, you will get as much done at school as possible and feel better by doing so. When you have appointments — perhaps your own kids to pick up and errands to run — and you cannot use those two hours for work, you will have to take your work home. All you can do is try to schedule everything around that time and use the time to leave your evenings work-free and stress-free.

Organizing

Being organized means it will take you less time to achieve more tasks. If you file papers as you finish them, you will not have that hanging over your head at the end of each day, and your desk will remain clear, making it easier to find what you need. Mark your calendar and keep it nearby so you can remember what is coming up and can be prepared.

These are ways to get through the daily grind without taking home the stress of your work. If you use these suggestions, you will enjoy your job more than other people do. One suggestion is instead of putting off a two- or three-minute task here and there throughout the day, take care of it right away. If you have eight of those tasks at the end of the day, you are adding an extra half-hour to the time you will already be staying after school. Another way to save time is to deal with the mail right away. If it is junk, throw it out instead of setting it aside to look it over later. If it is a piece of mail that requires a response, do it right away.

You will find that schedule changes and interruptions can fill your day, leaving little to no time to take care of the many demands you already have on your plate. This is why being organized, prioritizing, and being consistent with your routine will help you throughout the year. Not only will you be thankful you have the free time at home, but you will find that you will be a much happier and effective teacher, and your students will enjoy your company. Another way to help you survive the daily grind is finding a mentor.

Finding a Mentor

Having a mentor is important in your line of work. There will be times when you will want questions answered, help, ideas, or simply someone to talk to.

CASE STUDY: TIPS FROM VETERAN TEACHERS

Jennifer Sherrill, Second-grade teacher
Sunrise Elementary
Palm Bay, Florida

Merrisa Herman, First-grade teacher
Shumaker School
Bellevue, Ohio

"As soon as I began, I was introduced to my mentor," said Jennifer Sherrill. "She was such a blessing to have in the midst of my new job and the many questions that poured out of me. We attended numerous workshops together and even car pooled to them. This time served as a great opportunity for a question-and-answer session, plus I was able to ask about how to use the materials in my classroom whenever I was stuck. I believe that this (mentorship) is a wonderful program for new teachers, as it gives them a guarantee for at least one person to go to for all those little questions and road blocks that we encounter — not to mention the mounds of advice that they provide."

Merrisa Herman, a teacher with five years' experience, said she still contacts her mentor when she has questions or is in need of something. "I had a great mentor," she said. "I got lots of ideas and techniques from her that I use in my classroom today. I could not have made it through my first year without her. She made me feel at ease and was always there to help me with lessons and ideas."

Some school districts have mentors for their beginning teachers, while others do not. If you are beginning a new job without a mentor, begin looking for a teacher who has a lot of experience teaching and enjoys his or her job. You will know this teacher by his or her sincerity and good attitude. This teacher will have no problem being observed by other teachers. A good mentor will be excited to share ideas and knowledge with you, and this person will be someone who is enthusiastic about teaching.

The best way to find a mentor is to try to observe how the teachers in your school interact with their students. He or she will be more than willing to listen to your concerns about curriculum issues, where to find materials for activities, what administration and parents expect of you, how to work with the parents in your community, and how to create good lesson plans. There will never be too many questions for an effective mentor to answer, and he or she will never make you feel uncomfortable for coming to them for help.

While it is true some veteran teachers do not like beginning teachers, there are just as many who are enthusiastic about helping a new staff member. Try not to let the distance some veteran teachers seem to keep affect you. For many veteran teachers, it is not that they do not like you personally, it is that they have a "wait and see" approach, and sometimes even a type of safeguard against new teachers. This safeguard is in place because they do not want to make friends with someone who may leave before the year is over. Because a large percentage of rookie teachers end up leaving the profession, there are veteran teachers who choose not to get close until they see if the new teacher has what it takes to stick it out and stay with the job.

The importance of your mentor cannot be overstated. You will be overwhelmed with the daily demands, piles of paperwork, periodic meetings, and insurmountable memos. These are the things you will need to talk about with someone who has experienced it. Your mentor will understand what you are feeling, and you will know your mentor survived what you are now going through.

If you hear of another new teacher in the building, you may want to find him or her and introduce yourself. No one understands what you are experiencing better than someone who is going through the same thing. It will give comfort to both of you when you need it most, encouragement when you feel like quitting, humor when outsiders do not understand, and feedback when it cannot be found anywhere else. There will be times when your profession will make you feel isolated and lonely, and having another beginning teacher to discuss these feelings with will greatly ease that discomfort.

Teacher Mentoring Programs

Inexperienced teachers sometimes want to know who becomes a mentor and why. That is a question Florida's Brevard County public school leaders have answered. Brevard County's school system has a principal leadership program and a teacher induction program, and both have proved to be successful. In Brevard County schools, all new teachers go through the induction program and are mentored by a veteran teacher.

So who are these people who become mentors? According to Brevard County schools, they are "high-performing, experienced teachers." These teachers are veterans who work closely with new teachers, guiding them while giving continuous coaching and constructive feedback. In Brevard County schools, mentors are expected to:

- Foster a supportive and positive relationship with mentored colleague(s).

- Participate in meetings and activities with the new teacher that introduces them to the school and faculty.

- Share knowledge, expertise, and constructive guidance.

- Conduct two formative observations.

- Act as primary resource for the new teacher and offer specific information.

One of the most important reasons for schools to have a teacher mentoring program is that studies have shown that mentoring teachers is related to retaining new teachers in the profession. The studies seem to indicate teacher mentoring programs are a key factor in convincing teachers to stay in the profession, and it is believed that the reason the program works is because new teachers do not feel so overwhelmed when there is a mentor to help them meet the job's demands. Making the workload more manageable is how mentors help the most, because the workload is the leading cause of stress in a new teacher's life.

The mentoring program for teachers also improves student achievement because new teachers get assistance in lesson planning, organization, and preparation. The biggest problem mentors face is the same problem all teachers face — lack of time. If possible, plan to meet with your mentor on a regular basis. There will be times this will not be possible, and as a fellow teacher who struggles to have enough time of your own, this should be perfectly understandable. Help your mentor by using e-mail or calling only in the evening. You might find that your mentor is a morning person, and you could meet for coffee and doughnuts before school once a week. There is also the possibility of car pooling, giving you time to talk on the way to school and again on the way home. This also leaves the time that you have set aside for the morning and afternoon free to accomplish tasks.

According to the National Education Association, "Evidence strongly suggests that mentoring improves the quality of teaching." Many schools are now in the second generation of the mentoring program. The first generation was a learning experience for all involved and, unfortunately, those first mentors were not trained, and it was sometimes an overwhelming experience for the veteran teachers as well as the new teachers. The longer we have mentors, the more we learn about what is needed by new teachers and students, and the better the mentors become. When the mentorship programs improve, so does the quality of the new teachers, and with effective teachers comes better achievement of the students.

The problems you will face in your first year of teaching will not all be solved when you have a mentor, but having one will help ease the discomfort brought on by those problems not solved right away. When you are feeling doubtful of remaining in the profession, a good mentor will point out your strengths, help you build a good dialogue with your students, and ease the headaches of whether your lesson plans need improvement. With continuous feedback on how to improve, you are certain to have a successful first year as an elementary teacher. And yet another factor that will help you have a successful first year teaching is knowing the mindset of your students.

Part Three:

Your Primary School Students

"*I have taken several classes and seminars on discipline and taken a little from each. I feel you need to be consistent and run a class with routine so children know what to expect every day. Nowadays, you may be the only consistent thing in their lives. I do a lot of positives with the children, individually and as a whole class, as an incentive for good behavior. Don't focus on bad behavior; reward the good. When you reward one child, they all try to receive the same reward. That is not to say [you should] ignore bad behavior. I believe in timeouts when needed, a minute per age of the child — my students receive five minutes. We talk a lot about good and bad choices, and what each will get you.*"

— *Malia Jarvis, kindergarten teacher at Shumaker School in Bellevue, Ohio*

Chapter 7

The Mindset of Your Primary Students

Working with young children is exciting and fun while watching them learn and grow, but it can also be trying. Young students normally feel some anxiety upon entering school for the first time, but will become more relaxed and free of their anxiety once they realize their teacher is not an ogre. Even older students feel some trepidation and worry about entering a new grade and having to get to know a new teacher, but these feelings will decrease with time. Your welcoming attitude and smiling face will likely make most of your students feel better right away.

CASE STUDY: TIPS FROM VETERAN TEACHERS

Jennifer Sherrill
Second-grade teacher
Sunrise Elementary
Palm Bay, Florida

Carol Baker
Third-grade teacher
Sunrise Elementary
Palm Bay, Florida

To help ease students' anxiety when starting school, Jennifer Sherrill finds that greeting students at the door is a wonderful way to start the day off right. "You can observe how they are feeling: Do they look sick, sad, happy, etc., and get tips for what to look for once the door closes," she said. "Throughout the day, I like to provide positive feedback and reassurance."

"There are endless ideas on how to build rapport, but the main idea is to get them to know you and let them know what you expect from them," Carol Baker said. "You want them to understand that you are a real person that went to school just like them and enjoy activities outside of school. You also want them to respect you as the adult and trust that you have their best interest at heart. I try to make them know that I care about them and that together we can have a great year full of learning."

Dealing With Student Shyness

When social expectations are new or unclear, it is typical for a child to be shy, timid, and even anxious. As you get to know your students, you will determine whether their shyness or withdrawal is part of their personality or due to the new environment they have entered. It has been suggested that having shy students work with younger children helps them gain confidence, and the same is said for peer involvement. Find out what subject your shy or withdrawn student excels in and have them help another student who may be experiencing some problems in that area. Pairing a shy child with an outgoing student may help the shy student feel more comfortable, and putting them in group activities can also help alleviate any discomfort they may feel when called upon to answer a question.

Another suggestion for helping a shy student feel more comfortable is to have them do special errands; this makes them feel you have confidence in their ability and therefore builds their confidence in themselves. Taking time to have conversations with shy or withdrawn students is another way to pull them out of their shell. Teacher intervention is especially important for these students.

There are some instances where a student's shyness goes beyond what is considered normal. Signs to watch for when you expect a child may be abnormally shy are:

- The child never speaks or talks only in a whisper

- The child does not ever use the restroom, usually because he or she is afraid to ask

- The student never eats lunch and claims he or she is not hungry

- The student always appears sad or withdrawn

- He or she becomes visibly anxious when called upon

- Rarely, if ever, does the child play with other children

- He or she looks at the ground when being spoken to

- He or she complains of stomachaches or headaches

If you notice a child with these symptoms, and the symptoms last months into the school year, you may want to speak with the parent about the possibility of counseling. Some parents can take such suggestions to heart and think you are insinuating that something is wrong with their child. Be sure to explain to the parents that you are concerned, that you care about their child, and that you only want them to be healthy and happy.

Coping with separation anxiety

Separation anxiety is another normal reaction for children when entering school or a new grade. This anxiety is most common in children between the ages of 5 and 7 and between the ages of 11 and 14. Approximately 10 to 15 percent of children experience separation anxiety at some time; the key is to help them control their emotions. Crying, throwing tantrums, clinging, or refusing to be left alone are some of the symptoms of separation anxiety. Other symptoms can include:

- Excessive fear of something happening to themselves or their parents

- Vomiting

- Diarrhea

- Sweating

- Stomachache

- Headache

- Shaking or trembling

- Rapid breathing

A child will experience one or two of these symptoms but will not realize what the problem is, making it more stressful for him or her. It is impossible for children to learn or retain lessons in school when they are experiencing separation anxiety. Home is where they are in their comfort zone, but they may not realize this is why they are feeling so anxious. If children are more prone to having separation anxiety, they are more sensitive and will become sick, depressed, or nauseous when left at school. When they return to school the next day, they remember how they felt the first day and experience the same symptoms again.

Most children adjust within a few weeks, so be patient. A few suggestions for dealing with separation anxiety are:

- **Remain calm.** If you become agitated, the child will sense this, and his or her anxiety will intensify.

- **Explain what is happening.** Understanding what they are feeling and why they may feel this way helps them to recognize it and not become consumed by these feelings.

- **Teach the child to calm him or herself.** Try to encourage him or her to do some deep breathing whenever he or she feels nervous.

Anxiety is common in childhood and can interfere with academic performance, as well as social skills and general well-being. Anxiety can contribute to school failure so it is important to help students get through these feelings. While it may be trying and disruptive for the class, it is something you will most likely have to deal with as a teacher.

Know Your Students

If you carry an attitude that is positive and full of good expectations while maintaining a friendly disposition, your students will realize you are the leader of the classroom and will follow your lead. As long as you realize what the children need to feel safe, you can give them a sense of security, as well as an exemplary education.

CASE STUDY: TIPS FROM VETERAN TEACHERS

Don Shinton, Fourth-grade teacher
Cheston Elementary
Easton, Pennsylvania

Carol Baker, Third-grade teacher
Sunrise Elementary
Palm Bay, Florida

David Diaz, Physical education teacher
Southern Lehigh Intermediate
Bethlehem, Pennsylvania

Don Shinton said he tries to ease his students' fears by discovering what they already know before he begins teaching. "You should do a pre-assessment. After you know what level they are at, you design lessons that will challenge them but allow them to experience success. I design some lessons to start with a learning web, and then we brainstorm ideas. Sometimes the brainstorm is done in small groups, whole groups, or as a two-partner team. Ultimately, we share the ideas as a class. It builds a common understanding in the classroom. This is especially helpful for classrooms where the children come from different backgrounds," Shinton said.

"One thing I like to do (at the beginning of the year) is show a slideshow as an intro with pictures of things I like and people that are in my life," said Carol Baker. "This can help them find similarities that we share, and the bonding can begin. Then I have them put together an 'all about me' poster at home and bring it in that Friday, and we get to share as a class; that way, they can talk about themselves and what means the most to them."

David Diaz said he begins the year by allowing students to feel no pressure in physical education. He tells his students, "Physical education is for fun, and effort is a major part. Winning and losing does not matter. Trying your hardest is something that everyone can do."

Your Students' Expectations

It is important you remember you are not the only one who has expectations. Some expectations your students may have are that you will:

- Be a good leader
- Act consistently
- Be fair
- Stay honest
- Have expectations of them
- Keep a good attitude

Be a good leader

Always remember you must be a leader, not a friend. If you try to be a friend, you will not maintain control of your class. Being a leader means expecting your students to know and follow certain rules, and also means you expect to be shown respect, which requires you give respect. As a teacher you will need to take each student and be equally understanding and helpful to each one.

Act consistently

Consistency is sometimes the hardest part of teaching. Everyone has bad days, but as a teacher you must somehow find it in yourself to put away the negativity and carry on a positive attitude in the classroom. It will be the bad days that will measure your consistency as a teacher because those days will test your patience. No one, no matter how hard they try, can make every day a good day. However, the less often you react in a negative way, the more understanding your students will be when it does happen. If your daily attitude is positive and your general demeanor normally happy, then when you do have a bad day and give a student an abrupt answer, you will find that when you apologize for the abruptness, it will be shrugged off or already forgotten.

Be fair

Never make the mistake of thinking a student is too young to know or understand the things you say or any difference in how you may treat your students. Adults make this mistake often, and children sense this prejudice. Remember to treat each of your students fairly. You cannot let Adelina go to the bathroom each time she asks but never give David the same courtesy. This is unfair treatment, and every student in the classroom will be aware of it. While it may be true that David takes too long and it is obvious he is wasting time, you should explain to him this will not be allowed and if it continues, he will not be able to go to the restroom as often. By explaining this rule, you are maintaining leadership and at the same time giving David a fair warning. Your students will realize this and respect you for it.

Stay honest

Being honest does not mean you have to answer every question you are asked. There are some things that are not appropriate to discuss in class and you, as the adult, will be able to determine what those subjects are. This is especially true with older elementary students. Some teachers do not answer such questions as, "Do you drink?" while other teachers may answer, "In moderation," but this can be a touchy subject. However, if there are questions that arise during conversation, if you answer, you must remember to be honest.

Have expectations

It is all right to have expectations of your students; it is your job. You expect them to follow rules, cooperate, do their best, and learn what you teach. By having expectations, giving the consistency children need, and showing respect, you students will want to meet your expectations. It is also how students know that you believe in their abilities.

Keep a good attitude

By having a good attitude, you will show your students social skills. Positive reinforcement is contagious, and the students in your class will follow you by carrying the same kind of attitude you carry. Negativity breeds negativity, and you do not want to have a classroom full of negative kids.

Now that you have an idea of the expectations of your students, let us get to know your students and learn to understand them a little better.

Working With Your Students

If you give your profession your very best, your students will give their education the best they have. An adjustment many teachers need to make in their first year of teaching is to learn to keep their voice low and soft at all times. When you become frustrated because some students are acting out, it is important you remember to stay calm. If you try to out-scream 30 voices, you will find that the louder you scream at your students, the louder they will become. You must establish the fact that you are the leader to start and end the year with control of your classroom.

It is true the calmer and quieter you are when trying to get your students' attention, the faster they respond. Use body language, which is what effective mothers do when their kids are getting out of line. You can also try any of the following:

- Become silent and still, then make eye contact with the students who are acting out.

- Continue your lesson in a calm, quiet voice and walk over to stand very close to the student who is making the noise or causing the disruption.

- Become silent and still, raise your hand, and wait as one by one, your students do the same.

Starting on the very first day of class, you should be yourself. It is a bad idea to start the year pretending you are a strict and unbending teacher. It does not take long for the truth to show through, and the students will not only figure it out, but they will distrust you and run right over you. If you stay true to yourself, the rest of your year will be very successful.

The best advice you will ever receive when it comes to dealing with kids is to let your sense of humor show. Children will love your sense of humor and respond to it immediately with laughter, happiness, and trust. There are probably few professions that are as open to humor as teaching. Hopefully you will laugh with your students often in your first year of teaching, which is one of the ways you can connect with your students.

Connecting With Your Students

Getting to know your students will help you connect with them. It is not possible to connect with someone you know nothing about, even if you see them every day. Connecting with your students is the most important step you will take in helping your them achieve success.

There is a fall-out that comes with not connecting with your students, and it can be like a black cloud hanging over your head. Failing to connect will affect their success, which could cause guilt, regret, and stress for you as a new teacher. Building a good relationship with your students is like building any good relationship: It will take patience, work, kindness, understanding, and commitment.

Saying you should connect with your students and build a relationship does not mean you should get emotionally involved. Becoming emotionally involved can be very dangerous and can cause you to lose your ability to treat your students equally. By keeping an emotional distance, you will always give each of your students what they need, not what they want. Remember, it is your job to be their teacher; their peers will become their friends. Veteran teachers Tina Caldarelli and Don Shinton agree, saying it is most important to be there for your students — but you must also be a disciplinarian at all times.

CASE STUDY: TIPS FROM VETERAN TEACHERS

Don Shinton, Fourth-grade teacher
Cheston Elementary
Easton, Pennsylvania

Tina Caldarelli, Second-grade and
emotional support teacher
Cheston Elementary
Easton, Pennsylvania

Don Shinton agrees that discipline is important while still being a confidant for your students. However, the rules must be set and abided by. "If the class develops a set of rules that they are involved in creating, you get a greater by-in from the students, which allows you to be a moderator instead of a disciplinarian. I'm not sure that you should be a friend to your students. You want them to know that you care about them, and you want them to respect you. You can do this by creating a classroom environment where they can experience success and by setting up guidelines that make your classroom safe."

Tina Caldarelli said it is important that you always let your students know you care about them. Both teachers agree it is all right to let them know that you care about what they think and how they feel because this will help build the bridge to a good relationship. When your students know you care, they will trust you and listen to your lessons because they will want to live up to your expectations. Caldarelli said she is sure to "treat them all alike, and (I) am fair and firm. I am not afraid to give consequences and am very consistent with that. If they become extra friendly and ask personal questions, I explain to them that I am their teacher and they are the student, and that it is not appropriate. It is very easy to become emotionally attached to some students, especially knowing some of their backgrounds. However, the best thing for a teacher to do is offer them a safe, nurturing, and structured environment, for your classroom may be the only structure they may encounter in their lives."

Show your students you are in charge

The first step to connecting with your students is to assume a leadership role in your classroom from the first day of school. This will eliminate the possibility of someone else in your classroom, such as a student, attempting to gain the role of leader, which does sometimes happen with older elementary students. It is important your students have a voice in your classroom, but you are and should always be the one in control.

Here are some disciplinary steps you can implement in your classroom:

1.   **Give a reminder first** — This can be done for one or two students, or for the whole class. Giving a reminder is also giving the benefit of the doubt. By doing this, you are letting the student(s) or the class know that you realize they may have

forgotten the rules or it slipped their mind. This is also a way to, and the time to, stop the problem before it escalates.

2. **Give a warning** — By warning the student(s) or class, you are now giving a reprimand. A warning for a student should not be said across the room, but instead directly from you to him or her. Approach the student and tell him or her what they are doing wrong. Ask the student what he or she needs to do to correct this problem. By moving into the student's space, you are showing your authority and lack of tolerance for their misbehavior.

3. **Give a written warning** — The written warning should have the offensive behavior printed out and be sent home with the student to be signed by parents. If the student does not return the paper, he or she will be sent to the office. Remind the student of the next step in disciplinary action.

4. **Send the problems student to the office** — The student has now used every available option he or she has been given. Further action will be taken by agreement between you and the principal.

Do not worry that the first day of school will dictate the rest of the year. The day does not have to flow perfectly to ensure the rest of the year will be a good one. However, you do want to set a pace for being the leader on the first day. While it is important your students know you are the one in charge, there is a simple trick to making this happen. You are the teacher and it is your room; therefore, you should be in the room before anyone else appears. By this simple act, you are asserting the classroom is your territory. It is just as important that you are the last one in the classroom to establish the fact that you are the person in charge and the classroom is your domain.

The rules you set should be the rules you stick to; this will make the rest of your year much easier when it comes to teaching. By the second or third month of school, rather than wasting your time with asserting discipline, you will be able to focus on teaching because the class will already know your rules are to be followed. First-grade teacher Merrisa Herman said it is important students know what you expect. "All my students know what my expectations are," she said. "I tell them that we can have fun, but we also have to learn. Learning is our job when we are at school. My students understand that I'm their friend and that I make them follow school and classroom rules so everyone can learn and be safe."

New beginnings —
How to handle the first day

You will want to have the first day planned so there is little time for extraneous conversation or disruption. Your students will have a lot of questions, but the first day may not be the appropriate time to tackle all of them. It would be fine to have ten minutes at the beginning or the end of the day for questions, but you will not want to have questions interrupting the day. This also depends on the age of your students. Younger students are usually less disruptive on the first day because they are unsure of their new surroundings.

What should you do on the first day of school? You could begin by introducing yourself and then having your students introduce themselves, which helps them get over the nervousness of not knowing their peers. Another task for the day is highlighting some of the rules in your classroom. You may want to go over a list of rules and talk with the students about them to ensure the rules are understood. Discussing any emergency procedures is always a good idea with young students because it will help them understand there will be practice drills and they should not panic or be afraid.

Here is a possible breakdown of how a teacher can break the ice on the first day of school. Remember: This will vary according to your school's hours and your preferences, but it is a good general way to get started. For older students, you will want to make necessary changes:

- *8:00 a.m.* — Greet each student and his or her parent(s) at the door with a smile. When you introduce yourself, remember to bend down or squat so you are at the child's eye level. This brings comfort to a child.

- *8:30 a.m.* — When the class is settled in their seats, introduce yourself again and have each student share something about themselves such as their favorite game.

- *9:00 a.m.* — Play a simple but fun game that promotes sharing information as this is a good way to learn more about your students. For example, you can start the game with "I have…" and have each student finish the sentence with something, such as "a dog."

- *9:45 a.m.* — This is a good time for a light snack. If this becomes a daily routine, you may want to ask the parents to take turns sending a snack for the class.

- *10:00 a.m.* — Time to go over the school rules. Make it simple and talk about them with your students.

- *10:15 a.m.* — Time to go over rules for your classroom. Be sure you ask for student input.

- *10:30 a.m.* — As a class, recite what the students should know: colors, numbers, alphabet, etc.

- *11:00 a.m.* — This is a good time for writing practice and will help you assess your students. A good writing practice would be to have them write their name, address, and/or phone number.

- *11:30 a.m.* — Lunch and recess.

- *12:30 a.m.* — This is a good time to make sure the students have supplies they will need.

- *12:45 a.m.* — Go over where the supplies or study areas are in your classroom.

- *1:00 a.m.* — Read a short story to your class and encourage them to talk about it after it is finished. For older students, have them take turns reading.

- *1:15 a.m.* — A short recess is good here because young students get restless.

- *1:30 a.m.* — Give a short and fun homework assignment, preferably one that will help you assess your students, and have students return any supplies to appropriate area. Pass out papers to go home for parents.

- *2:00 a.m.* — Make sure all students put lunch boxes, homework assignments, and papers for home in their backpacks. As they line up for parent pick-up or the school bus, stand at the door with a smile and tell each student good-bye.

There will be a stack of paperwork for the students to take home for their parents to fill out. If you have a letter of introduction to your classroom for the parents of your students, send it home with this pile of paperwork.

The letter should introduce you as their child's teacher and give a bit of information about your credentials and your philosophy or goal for your students.

This letter should contain the following information:

- The date and time of Back to School night or Open House

- How often you intend to give homework

- What the students can expect the first few weeks of school

- A list of classroom rules

- Assurance that communication with parents is important to you for the sake of your students' education

Be sure to tell the students when this paperwork needs to be turned in, but give them time. Remember that parents work and are no happier than you are to see a pile of papers to fill out, especially if they have more than one child.

With elementary students, it is important that they know you are there to help them. Reassure them that you will be glad to help them if they do not understand a lesson or if they are confused. It is important to give all students this reassurance no matter their age, but younger children are sometimes afraid to ask for help.

There are ways to help younger students feel comfortable on the first day of school and some suggestions are:

- Talk to them about rules they had the previous year (or at home if they are kindergartners) and discuss how some of your rules are similar.

- Have the students point out objects in your room that they had last year or have at home, such as a clock, a desk, or plants.

- Read to your students to help eliminate their nervousness.

The point of these suggestions is to find similar objects or rules that they are already familiar with. By pointing out things they are familiar with, they will be more comfortable and not feel like they are in strange territory. By starting the first day in control of your classroom and with plans to put your students at ease, it will be a good start for your first year as a successful elementary teacher.

Managing Your Classroom Means Managing Your Students

You have learned that showing control to your students will help you gain their respect and trust, and it will also help you manage your classroom throughout the year. Part of managing your classroom is having a positive discipline plan, which entails giving encouragement for good behavior rather than focusing on bad behavior. Doing this is as much for your student's well-being as it is for your own. Your students will have more success in a classroom with little or no disruption, and a positive discipline arrangement will help you achieve that environment. Veteran teacher Jennifer Sherrill insists that discipline is important for all children, especially in a school environment.

CASE STUDY: TIPS FROM
VETERAN TEACHERS

Jennifer Sherrill
Second-grade teacher
Sunrise Elementary
Palm Bay, Florida

Jennifer Sherrill said that elementary students want to be your best friend. "However, they need you to set the boundaries and provide that structure that they crave," she said. "Make sure that you have some personal space that they know is only for you. Also, make sure that you are enforcing the rules to everyone and not bending them for a select few."

Developing a system for discipline

If you inform your students of the rules and consequences from the beginning of the year and stick to your rules, you will find your students to be cooperative and anxious to learn. A common mistake with new teachers is they are so worried about keeping the disruptive students in line that they forget to acknowledge the students who do follow the rules. This causes the good students to wonder why they bother being good because there is no positive reinforcement.

Depending on the age of your students, you will want your rules to be few and basic, with little room left for misinterpretation. It is a good idea to limit yourself to five or six rules. One good way to pique your students' interest for knowing the rules is allowing them to guess what the rules might be. Children enjoy guessing games, and it becomes a competition to see who can out-guess the others. It is also a good idea to ask the students for input on the rules or if they can think of any different or additional rules you may have overlooked. Students love having input and will surprise you with their suggestions. With older elementary students, this is sometimes a good opener for humorous antidotes and an icebreaker on that dreaded first day of school.

Using positive reinforcement

Positive reinforcement is important because it gives an example of what is socially and individually rewarded and acknowledged. As you give positive reinforcement to students who remember to raise their hand before speaking or follow other classroom rules, you are teaching the other students lessons about discipline as well as boosting the self-esteem of those who follow the rules.

A good habit to get into at the beginning of the year is to find a reason to praise each of your students every day, which will boost their self esteem, help them learn to trust you, and motivate them to succeed. Most students thrive on public praise, but keep in mind that there are some children who become embarrassed by public praise. These students are the ones you will want to praise in a quiet, private way, letting them know that you have learned who they are and that you respect their individuality. A quiet way of praising such a student could be simply setting a graded paper with praising comments on their desk or having the student last in line for recess so you can quietly praise them on the way outside.

A way to offer positive reinforcement is by offering rewards or badges for good behavior, depending on the age of your students. Another good idea is having a student of the week, possibly making a bulletin board or using a section of wall to display the student's success. Some teachers send a letter home or make a phone call to the parents so the students can share their moment in the limelight.

Dealing with problem students

Even with positive reinforcement, you will have a few students who will act out in a negative way, which is why you have a discipline plan in place. It is best if small offenses have small consequences. If a student steals an eraser, it would be best to have the student return the eraser to the owner with an apology rather than suspend him or her. However, a persistent problem with theft would require the larger consequence of suspension. Obviously the punishment for a student who forgets to raise his or her hand before speaking should not receive the same consequence as a student who starts a fire in the bathroom.

When it comes to your discipline arrangement, the most important factor is consistency. When your students know you will not sway, they will better follow the rules you have set in place. Remember that you will be expected to enforce school policy as well as your own classroom rules. Be sure you are up to date on the school policies, and ensure your rules fall in line with the overall school goals.

What you have already done in your classroom in preparation for the year will determine your ability to manage your classroom. Everything from the decorations to the bulletin boards and the seating arrangement will help you control what happens in your room. Your classroom is an inviting place where students can learn at ease as long as they follow your rules. Every one of your students is an individual, and some will test the waters right away, while others may test you all year long. *Chapter 9 will discuss some of the students who may test your patience more than others.*

Remember that it is far easier to prevent problems than it is to deal with them and the possible aftermath that could come with them. By showing your students you care, you will prevent many problems from arising.

When parents discipline a child they love, punishment is usually the last resort; the same policy should be applied in the classroom. A teacher who is a tyrant and attempts to make his or her students fear him or her to control them may go so far as to use physical contact out of anger. Using this tactic, it is only a matter of time before severe backlash will follow, and the teacher will be removed from his or her position.

When you have your students in a routine of entering the room, putting away their belongings, turning in homework, and picking up their area before going home, you are teaching them self-discipline. As you watch your students become more comfortable and sure of this routine, you will know you are creating the best learning environment possible and managing your classroom as you should. There will be days when you will be reminded that children still need to be guided and given discipline, but that is normal, and a gentle reminder is usually all that is required. From the beginning, you are simply teaching your students to manage their behavior. This frees you to concentrate on teaching effectively and helps your students learn how to become assets to their community. By being what your students need, you will help them become successful in school. As a teacher, you are more than just an educator; you are a solid foundation and a positive role model.

Chapter 8

More Than an Educator: Being What Your Students Need

As an elementary school teacher, you will learn that some of your students have emotional baggage they always carry with them — and sometimes the result of that baggage is seen in the classroom. As much as we might not like to admit it, there are children who are mistreated, neglected, abused, and sometimes held in contempt by their parents. These students will need more assistance than you alone can give, and there will be other adults who will step in, such as the school counselor. You will probably not be able to detect who these children are on the first day, but with time, you will discover which ones are in need.

There are also students who may not be physically abused, but may simply be in need of an adult who cares. The best way to help these students deal with some of their problems is to help them build self-esteem. Simply showing your students you care is the most important step in helping them gain self-esteem.

You will quickly learn that you are much more than just an educator. You will find yourself playing many roles, and the following list is just a few of the roles that you will become familiar with:

- Surrogate parent
- Confidant
- Social worker
- Provider
- Doctor
- Psychologist
- Cheerleader
- Referee
- Emergency worker

The Surrogate Parent

In addition to teaching your students, it is also your job to keep them safe, nurture them, discipline them, instruct them on manners, and teach them social skills. You will meet all these needs while the students are in your care, making you their surrogate parent while they are in your classroom.

The Confidant

By being a child's confidant, you are being his or her friend, and unfortunately, you may be the only adult in that student's life who cares. This means you will be there for them if something arises while they are in your care, but you also can expect certain responsibilities to be performed while in your care. If you suspect Heather is being neglected at home, you will make sure the correct authorities are informed, but she will still be expected to do the school work while in class. You must be careful to not cross the fine line of confidant/authoritarian. It is good to let your students know you care and want to talk with them, praise them, and encourage them, but always remain their teacher first.

The Social Worker

The social worker hat is the hat many teachers dread, but it is your respon-sibility as a teacher to make sure your students are being taken care of properly. If you overhear a student telling another child that they are afraid to go home because Mommy and Daddy are mean and hit them, it will be up to you to follow up on this child's well-being. You may notice welts or bruises on a student and if so, it is time to speak with the counselor at your school. There is some fallout that comes with this role, but it is some-thing you may have to do to ensure your student's safety. Also remember to always keep your principal informed of such problems. To leave him or her out of the loop would be a drastic mistake because it will make him or her look bad as the leader of the school, and possibly may jeopardize your job. If the principal unexpectedly has an irate parent show up in the office in a confrontational mode, he or she is going to wonder if it was a mistake hir-ing you. The leader of your school should always be an informed leader. As of 2009, all 50 states had passed some form of mandatory law on reporting child abuse and neglect in order to qualify for the Child Abuse Prevention and Treatment Act (CAPTA) funding, which totaled more than $109 mil-lion at the beginning of 2009. Every state has a hotline for reporting abuse and neglect, and all states require teachers to report their knowledge or suspicions to a law enforcement authority or child protection agency.

The Provider

Being a temporary provider is something you will find yourself doing often. There will be occasions when a student may forget his or her lunch money, and it is not uncommon for a teacher to cover this cost. You may notice some of your students do not have a winter coat or gloves, and you might take it upon yourself to try to help them out. Just be careful with this role because it is possible the student or the student's parents may become insulted or embarrassed. An example of how you could do this would be to call the parent or speak to him or her if they pick his or her child up after school. Kindly say that you noticed Kurt had not been wearing his gloves and may have lost them. Then tell the parent that you happened to have an extra pair that had belonged to your nephew, and you would like to know if it is all right if you give them to Kurt.

The Doctor

Wearing the doctor hat can happen in different ways. When your students know you care, and they trust you, they are going to want to turn to you when they are hurt. It is natural for this to happen, and it simply means you are an effective teacher. It is also your responsibility to watch for any communicable diseases such as ringworm or lice. This kind of problem can spread quickly, and it is up to you to be on the lookout for any problems of this nature. Be sure to alert your school nurse immediately; protocol requires the nurse to call the parent.

The Psychologist

This role is necessary when you realize something such as a child's shyness is beyond average. This does happen, and it is best to try to help the child by giving a lot of praise and encouragement. You may have a child who becomes aggressive, and it will be up to you to ensure the student gets help. You will want to speak with the guidance counselor or school nurse and the principal, and if you are unsure of what to do, ask your mentor, a veteran teacher, or your principal. The child may need counseling or anger management; however, this will not be your decision to make. Again, it is best to keep your principal informed of any situation that could become a problem. As an effective teacher, you will know, or at least have concerns about, this problem being beyond your capacity for control, and you will meet with your principal to discuss what should be done in that situation. If this is the case, the principal will most likely remove the child from your classroom and place the student in another class.

As a teacher, you should watch for any student who becomes agitated or suddenly withdraws. Also watch for signs of depression, such as mood swings or sudden anger. These are red flags that signal there is an emotional problem, and they will need to be attended to. Once you speak with the parents, you may find that the child's favorite grandparent has passed away, or Mom and Dad are getting a divorce. If possible, try to keep the parents involved because it is best to have some knowledge of what is going on that caused the change in the student's behavior.

The Cheerleader

As a teacher, it is imperative you give your students praise and encouragement. Even when a student does an average job, acknowledge the effort of that student and encourage him or her to keep trying to improve. This is your cheerleading hat, and it is one that you will wear all the time. Remember that even the students who always do well need praise and encouragement. Do not forget about them because they are good students.

The Referee

You will also have to referee some disagreements, but you must do this with finesse and diplomacy. You cannot take sides unless the offense is extreme, and it is clear who the offender is. If you witness an offense, you will give consequential punishment. If you are unsure of what took place, it is best to speak with the parties involved separately, but in a way that is calm and never accusatory. If you have a student come to you with a visual wound, such as a black eye, and you witnessed the student being hit by another student, you would certainly be justified in taking a side and enacting rules against fighting.

Do not forget that all children lie at times, and you will not always be able to tell who is being truthful. This is the type of situation that must be handled carefully because you do not want to damage the trust your students have put in you. If the offense is minimal, such as a heated argument, you will want to give light punishment, especially if you are unsure of who started the offensive behavior. If the offensive behavior is harsh, such as physical fighting, you will want the consequences to be more severe. Keep in mind that one of the parties involved may be innocent and forced to protect himself or herself. If this is something you suspect as true, the answer to consequences may fall between minimal and harsh, such as extra homework along with no recess, no library time, and eating lunch alone for a set period of time. As always, this will vary with the age of your students.

Whether a student is lying can be hard to determine, but it will become easier as you get to know your students as individuals.

The Emergency Worker

Wearing the hat of an emergency worker is a job you may hope you never experience. Even if you never don this hat, you must still be ready for the day it may happen. Fires, tornadoes, hurricanes, blizzards, bomb threats, and any other disastrous situation will require you to wear the hat of the emergency worker. Be sure you are familiar with your school's emergency procedures because if something happens, your students' safety will depend on your ability to follow through.

The many hats you wear are what make you an effective teacher. While it may seem impossible to fulfill many different roles simultaneously, it is not. For parents, this is everyday life. For teachers who are not parents, it may take some time to become proficient at this, but it will happen. As long as you sincerely care about your students, the rest will follow. And just as parents lead by example, teachers understand they must teach by example.

Teach by Example

Being a teacher can be scary, and it carries tremendous responsibility. In today's society, many children are basically left on their own, lacking adult attention and encouragement, not to mention the direction they need to make the right choices. You may be the only adult who will show them care and concern, and it might be up to you to show them how to have manners, good character, and self-discipline.

When the school has a guest speaker who gives a talk about the dangers of drugs, this may be the first time some children have heard this message. This may be hard to believe, but it is true that some parents do not talk with their children about such dangers in life. You, as a teacher and a role model, can and should reinforce the right messages when appropriate.

How you speak, how you address people in all walks of life, and all of your actions will have an influence on your students. When you help your students learn how to control their anger or stay organized, you are influencing their character. When you show appreciation, sympathy, or concern, you are teaching your students social skills. Every time you laugh at yourself, treat others with respect, and accept criticism gracefully, you are leading by example and being an effective teacher and positive role model.

However, there are times that even an effective teacher has run-ins with a parent.

School Versus Home

What students learn in school, whether it is something they learn from the teacher or hear from their peers, can sometimes be a touchy subject with some parents. There are certain topics that have become controversial or are emotional for parents, including holidays, sex education, and religion. It is possible that you may find your own personal convictions stepped on by what you are required to teach.

Instead of being offended by what may seem to be an off-handed way to teach something important to him or her, an effective teacher knows to overlook personal matters and teach what the school requires in an educational and unbiased way. Be aware that your curriculum may be questioned by some parents, and you may be verbally attacked for teaching these lessons, such as the history of some Bible characters versus religious beliefs. Some parents are deeply steeped in their religious beliefs and will be offended if the history lesson merely teaches that Jewish people were once slaves. These parents may feel you should embellish and take the lesson further, delving into talk of religious morals. Another example is sex education, which some districts approach with older elementary students. Some parents believe this is strictly their job and none of the school's business. In some districts, it is required that parents be informed of this "talk," and they then have the opportunity to pull the child from that particular program. As long as you are carefully following the set standards and curriculum, your principal should support you, and you can assure the parents that you are following district and state laws.

Some of the subjects and holidays that can cause parental concern are:

- Halloween
- Pledge of Allegiance
- December holidays
- Martin Luther King Jr. Day
- Easter
- Sex education
- Religion
- Alcohol
- Tobacco
- Black History Month
- School violence

Some of these subject areas are self-explanatory as to why they may cause controversy with parents; sex education is one such subject. There are parents who feel the schools have overstepped their boundaries on this matter, stating that it is their job as parents to teach this subject matter to their children.

Saying the Pledge of Allegiance is not allowed for some students due to their parents' religious beliefs, and this is something you as a teacher must be prepared for. While parents have every right to expect their children to abide by their rules, they sometimes do not understand the predicament they are putting their child in. For instance, if a student's parents tell you he or she is not allowed to say the Pledge of Allegiance, the student is going to feel different compared to his or her classmates. As an effective teacher, it will be up to you to try and remedy that problem and ease the child's discomfort. There are several ways you can do this, depending on the age of your class.

- When questioned by a student about why Carlos does not have to participate in the Pledge of Allegiance, explain that there are many different kinds of religions and Carlos' family's religion does not allow him to participate.

- Use the opportunity to have a class discussion about the diversity of people, cultures, and religion. You can veer the conversation away from Carlos and have the class back into learning a lesson within a few minutes.

- Have Carlos run errands while the class says the Pledge of Allegiance. He could take the lunch count or absenteeism slip to the proper office, or maybe return library books.

Because religion is an emotional subject for some families, it is good practice to avoid this subject if possible. There are some states that have religious subject matter in their history books and, depending on the age of your class, it is suggested that you teach this curriculum as is and move on.

There are going to be times that controversial subjects will come up in the classroom. A child may begin to repeat a parent's negative opinion on different cultures, and this can be a controversial subject, depending on the age of the students and where the conversation leads. If the subject is one that is inappropriate or prejudicial, such as explicit talk of sex or racial slurs, it is best to stop the discussion as soon as it begins.

Politics is another hot topic that can cause parents to become upset and should be handled with care. Depending on your students' ages, it can be a prime opportunity for learning, especially if there is an election taking place. You could hold an election in your classroom and use this opportunity to teach your students about how our government works. However you decide to use such an event, be sure it is only in an unbiased and educational way for your students to learn.

School violence is a scary subject for some students, and there are teachers who have a difficult time dealing with this subject. Regardless of if you are one of these teachers, it is best if you have some facts on the subject in case your students bring it up. It is also a good idea to have some suggestions about what students can do to help prevent school violence from happening. The Centers for Disease Control and Prevention has a Web site full of resources for teachers who talk with their students about school violence. You can find this Web site at **www.cdc.gov/ViolencePrevention/youthviolence/schoolviolence/index.html**.

Another controversial subject is prejudice, and you will need to teach your class that prejudices are unacceptable. Teaching your students to respect one another and showing respect for each of your students is the best way to do this. Explaining the diversity in people from other countries, how America was built on diversity, and how we all live together peacefully is a good way to teach acceptance. It is also the best way to teach about prejudices without having to discuss the minute details of this subject.

Be prepared for some awkward questions or inappropriate language during some holidays. Like it or not, there are still people who are prejudiced and will voice these feelings in front of their children. You may hear a child repeat a negative comment about how his or her parents do not want the student to be friends with someone who does not celebrate Christmas. Some parents will even demand that their children have the same biased views as they do. This may cause a child to question your lessons, and you need to have unbiased, logical answers ready for such an occasion.

If your priority is the education and well-being of your students while they are under your care, most of your possible parent problems are already solved. Most parents want their children to receive a good education, and knowing your heart is in the right place will ease any distrust they would otherwise have. There could be problems with parents in other areas, and sometimes behavior problems in your students can be what will stir up the hornet's nest. Just remember to maintain a positive attitude and keep the parents informed.

This next chapter will describe how you can work with your students' parents to help the children in your classroom succeed.

Chapter 9

Working With Parents and Students With Behavior Problems

By involving the parents on the first day of school, you are opening the door for good communication as well as setting the standards for what you expect from their children. Even more importantly, you are forming a team and giving your students what they need most for a successful education: parental involvement.

It is a fact that students who have involved parents are more successful in their education. Speak with teachers, principals, and psychologists, and they will all tell you this is true. There have been many studies done to show the difference in students with involved parents and those without, such as the American Education Research Association study titled "1997 Review of Educational Research." Parental involvement is important for your students and for you because when parents are left out of the loop, distrust and hard feelings can occur. The Michigan Department of Education agrees with the "1997 Review of Educational Research" and cites research about parental involvement in their child's education. The research shows:

- The earlier in a child's education the parents become involved, the more powerful the effect.

- The most effective form of parent involvement takes place when parents work directly with children on learning activities at home.

- Eighty-six percent of the general public believes support from parents is the most important way to improve the schools.

- The biggest problem facing the schools is lack of parental involvement.

- Decades of research show that parent involvement gives students:

  1. Higher test scores, graduation rates, and grades
  2. Better school attendance
  3. Increased motivation and better self-esteem
  4. Lower rates of suspension
  5. Decreased use of drugs and alcohol
  6. Fewer incidences of violent behavior

- Parent involvement in education is twice as predictive of student academic success as family socioeconomic status.

- The more intense parent involvement is, the more successful the achievement.

Regardless of whether your students are exceptional, average, or have problem areas, it is beneficial to all of your students to have parental involvement, and therefore it is beneficial to you as an effective elementary teacher.

CASE STUDY: TIPS FROM
VETERAN TEACHERS

Merrisa Herman, First-grade teacher
Shumaker School
Bellevue, Ohio

Tina Caldarelli, Second-grade and
emotional support teacher
Cheston Elementary
Easton, Pennsylvania

Tina Caldarelli said the most important way to earn a parent's trust and respect is through communication. "Take the time to write notes, e-mails, and make phone calls," she said.

Being professional is imperative, too, said Merrisa Herman. "If you have respect for peers, parents, students, and administration, then they will have respect for you," she said.

Meeting With Parents

Both students and teachers benefit from keeping parents informed, and this will also make your job much easier. When parents are informed, the students realize their parents and their teacher are allies. Rather than misbehave or buck the system that is made up of the most important adults in their life, the students will most likely work harder at being successful. Parents will jump to your defense and support you as a teacher as long as you keep them informed and maintain an open-door policy.

All schools offer opportunities for teachers and parents to meet. Usually these opportunities are Back to School night, Open House, or Teacher/ Parent Conferences. These events are an exceptional time to go over the class rules and give an overview of the goals for the year. This is also a prime opportunity to answer questions, sign up parents for volunteer work, and suggest some ways that parents can help their children with their education.

While you will have your concerns about your first year as a teacher, keep in mind you will want to appear confident and enthusiastic. This will relieve the parents who are worried about their child's new teacher. Most parents worry about their child's first year in school as well as the transition between grades and how their child will deal with the changes. When parents have questions, concerns, or suggestions, listen with your heart, and they will sense your sincerity. If they feel you are sincere, available, enthusiastic, and understanding, they will be won over at the beginning of the year.

Your mission for these events should be to show the parents that you care about their children and their education. You are also letting the parents know that you want them to be involved and that the door for communication is always open. This begins a mutual respect and trust between you and the parents, helping you become a more effective teacher and helping the parents know that it is all right to speak with you about any concerns they may have.

You school will schedule these conference dates, and most schools will schedule them at the end of the first quarter of the year or perhaps twice a year. Check with your administration to know your school's policy on conference nights. For these conferences, you should have a portfolio for each student with notes on the child's strengths and weaknesses. Share positives with the parents but follow up with any area the child might need to work on for improvement. If the child has made progress in certain areas, have some examples of this to share with the parents. Show parents the student's work from the beginning of the semester and more recent papers, such as practice papers or graded papers on writing.

Listen to the parents' concerns and hear their comments. Do not dismiss what they have to say because it could very well be something that can help you become a more efficient teacher in the following years. If a parent comes to you and points out that their gifted daughter who is in your class is struggling over so much homework, consider what he or she is saying. Perhaps you are expecting more than what is possible from your students. Never forget that in most cases, no one knows a child better than a parent.

It is in your best interest, the students' best interest, and the parents' best interest to be sure any problem is not left unattended until teacher/parent conferences. They should be aware of problems or difficulties before they walk into your room for the conference. If you keep parents informed throughout the year, they will be your allies. They will have a better chance of knowing if their child is trying to pull the wool over their eyes or outright lying to them about school. There are ways to keep parents informed throughout the year: You could write a newsletter once a week or once a month. Also, many teachers have an online syllabus or homework page. Either of these forms of communication could be used as reminders of upcoming reviews or tests.

Uncooperative Teachers

Some teachers would rather be submerged into boiling water than deal with parents or have parents involved with their class in any way. These teachers have either had a bad experience with a parent, or the teacher has heard horror stories and is now intimidated by the mere idea of a parental visit. While it is possible these teachers can be effective leaders, they are always viewed with distrust and contempt by parents who are in no way at fault. When parents sense a closed-door attitude, they will immediately dislike and distrust that teacher because of that attitude, and they are usually right to do so.

The teachers with the closed-door attitude are usually the type of teachers who think they are never wrong. It is these types of teachers who cause problems for other educators and give the profession a bad name. No matter how much experience you may have, there will be times you are wrong, which is why it is so important that you truly hear what parents say to you. Parents want what is best for their children, and it is your job and responsibility to want the same.

The biggest flaw teachers have is neglecting to contact a student's parents, according to parent surveys taken for the report "Teachers Talk: School Culture, Safety, and Human Rights," by Elizabeth Sullivan and Elizabeth Keeney. The No. 1 reason for this neglect is the absence of time. With all the demands teachers must meet, it is hard enough to do all that is necessary to be a good teacher. Trying to find the time to call a parent, advise them of a problem, and ask them to help is another task on the list. However, it is strongly suggested that you make the time to contact parents whose children are having more difficulties than other students. Prioritize the calls and place them from most difficult situations to less difficult. If a student is high risk for becoming a failing student, it is only logical that his or her parents are the ones who need to be contacted first. Smaller problems, such as Molly's persistence in wanting to be first in line, can wait their turn for the phone call. By taking the time to speak with these parents, you will most likely see improvement in the child's work or behavior. You will also have more parents cheering for you throughout the year.

Parents' Expectations of You

For the most part, parents want and expect the same things from you as their children do. The following is a list of some expectations parents have:

- Be fair
- Be caring
- Be consistent
- Keep them informed
- Keep their child safe
- Show respect
- Work with them
- Teach their child what he or she needs to know
- Make your class an enjoyable experience

To be a truly effective teacher, you should send home positive messages and not just make contact when something is wrong. Not only will the parents appreciate hearing positive news about their child, this will also help the students have good self-esteem. Be sure to keep a record of any contact with parents. If you send home a letter or classroom newsletter, keep a copy on file. If you make a phone call, record the date, time, and a brief overview of the conversation. Like it or not, the outcome can get messy with problem parents and it is always best to be prepared for a dispute or a complaint.

When you involve the parents in your students' education, you are increasing the chances of their success. In the 2008 report, "Teacher's Talk: School Culture, Safety, and Human Rights," 65 percent of teachers surveyed said they feel parental involvement would increase their students' academic success. Seventy-two percent of teachers believe students are more likely to fall through the cracks when there is not parental involvement. When parents are not involved, the end result is a child who feels he or she is not worthy of attention. This leads to students with low self-esteem and sometimes students with behavior problems.

Any words of encouragement or praise you give to a student can and will have a lasting impact on their future. This is easy enough to do when they are well-behaved students, but dealing with students who have behavioral problems may be a bit more challenging, which is why it is best to have an idea of how to handle some behavior problems before they happen.

How to Handle Behavior Problems

Behavior problems in students can cause a great deal of stress for the best of veteran teachers and can cause new teachers to want to quit the profession entirely. Inclusion practically guarantees you will have at least one student with a behavior problem, so it is best if you are prepared for this. The demands on teachers are already enormous, and the addition of a child or children with challenging behavior will play a role in how you react to any given situation. Patience is the key for most situations, but there is so much more than mere patience involved in dealing with students who have behavior problems.

So what exactly constitutes behavior problems? Challenging behavior is any behavior that interferes with a child's development. If a child has a problem controlling his or her anger, it is going to interfere with his or her education. A behavior problem can be harmful to a student, his or her peers, or adults the student interacts with. Challenging behavior puts a student at risk for failing school and having social problems in upcoming years. It has become common for teachers to receive students who need further assistance than the teacher is able to give. If you ever find yourself in such a situation, it is time to seek help. Speak with the principal and the special education teacher about this matter as soon as possible so the student can get the proper help and education needed.

If you have a child in your classroom who is acting out, what do you do to help this child? According to Barbara Kaiser and Judy Sklar Rasminsky, authors of *Challenging Behavior in Elementary and Middle School*, "Research about the brain and resiliency tells us that consistent, nurturing relationships are a child's best protection against risk, including the risk of challenging behavior." By connecting with students who are high risk and those who experience challenging behavior, you are giving them a better opportunity for a bright, healthy future. Veteran teachers Don Shinton, Carol Baker, and Tina Caldarelli realize how important it is to remember that even students with behavior problems can learn and succeed, and involving their parents is important.

CASE STUDY: TIPS FROM VETERAN TEACHERS

Don Shinton, Fourth-grade teacher
Cheston Elementary
Easton, Pennsylvania

Carol Baker, Third-grade teacher
Sunrise Elementary
Palm Bay, Florida

Tina Caldarelli, Second-grade and emotional support teacher
Cheston Elementary
Easton, Pennsylvania

Don Shinton believes that behavioral problems can be challenging: "Be proactive and contact parents for their help. Don't wait too long before calling. They know their children." Your relationship with these students is crucial, and it is essential that you create a bond, giving them a better chance to succeed academically and socially.

Tina Caldarelli was an emotional support teacher for six years and now teaches second grade. She advised to always be consistent when giving consequences.

"Make sure the students know the rules and the consequences. Have them posted in your room. Always follow through," she said.

Carol Baker said that it is necessary for behavior problems to be nipped as soon as possible."I know there are some kids who are behavior problems for every teacher they have ever had, but to keep yourself sane, you might need to think of something those other teachers haven't thought of and try something new," she said. "The best thing to do is find something that means something to them and allow them to work for it, whether it is time on the computer or extra recess time. All kids want to have something to work for, so you just have to find it."

She went on to tell a story about one of her behavior problem students. "I had one student who couldn't read and was a huge disruption if he was overwhelmed. I found out that he always told one of the first-grade teachers that he was learning to read in my class, and she would tell him to come read to her class one day. So, to get him to do his work during class, I would give him a passage that I would help him learn, and when all of his work was done, he could go read to her class. His confidence skyrocketed when he read them a short passage because he felt successful, and the kids looked up to him.

"He would come back, and he was so excited to do his work because he wanted to go read to them again and get that feeling one more time. Just finding what works for that particular child can help, and it may change 100 times throughout the year."

There are three things to remember when creating a relationship with these students:

- Understand yourself to see children with behavior problems more accurately

- Understand the children with behavior problems in order to be better equipped to help them

- Establish a relationship with children in order to give them a better opportunity for success

Understanding yourself

By understanding yourself and how you see a child with a behavior problem, you can reflect and determine if you need to alter your views to be a more effective teacher. Sometimes there are character clashes, and this can cause more harm than good. If this is the case, it is best to have the child removed from your classroom and placed with another teacher. There are times a teacher will resent having a student who causes disruption in his or her classroom. There are also teachers who feel resentment for high-risk students for what they consider as taking up valuable time that could be used for their regular students. These are problems that have come with inclusion in the classrooms.

While it is understandable that inclusion has put more demands on teachers, it is also understood that teachers must deal with the laws and be committed to all students. If you have a student whom you cannot have removed from your class, you are going to have to find a way to deal with this student. You may see a student as difficult, but if you look for the root cause of the reasons why this student is difficult, you will better understand the student and take a different approach in dealing with their personality. There may be times a student seems to be annoying for no apparent reason, especially if it is early in the school year and you do not know the student. Get to know your students so you can connect with your problem students. In doing this, you may find that this student has a learning problem. Perhaps he or she struggles with reading, which can cause problems in other subjects. Once this is discovered, you can speak with the parents about ways they can help; you may want to assign a tutor, give assignments that will better help the student with reading, or make time to read with the student yourself.

Understanding your special needs students

There have been problems with teachers who have special needs students or students who have behavior problems when the teachers do not know how to work with them. Let us look at an example of this potential problem:

There were a set of twins who started kindergarten, and one of them is autistic. The teacher had no experience in dealing with an autistic child, but the law required that she teach them. When the teacher from the classroom next door came into the room, the autistic child reached up to touch her bright, shiny pin. The child's teacher yelled at the student, and the student had a meltdown. Not only was the class disrupted, but the teacher was upset, and the parents were furious that she handled the situation so poorly.

This problem could have been prevented if the teacher had received some proper training in how to handle behavior problems for special needs children. It has quickly become apparent that while inclusion can be effective for the children, it was implemented before those in charge realized the effects it can have on some teachers and the repercussions it can create for the students. If this teacher had been informed that the child is attracted to shiny objects, she may have handled the problem differently. What was an "instant reaction" on the teacher's part was not the reaction that should have taken place. A calm movement of gently removing the child's hand from the teacher's pin while diverting the child's attention would have been the proper handling of this particular situation.

Today, all states require student teachers to take at least one course that can help prevent such problems, but one has to wonder how much damage has already been done. This is why it is so important for teachers to understand their special needs students. Without proper training while in school, the only way to possibly get a better understanding of the special needs student is to spend time with his or her family, which is difficult to do in most cases.

Ted Riecken, chair of the Association of British Columbia Deans of Education (ABCDE), said "every teacher education program offers at least one course in special education, and in many programs, more than one course is required." All 50 states and the District of Columbia require special education teachers to be licensed, but due to inclusion, regular education teachers who also deal with special needs students every day do not have to be licensed. This has created a stir and now school districts offer their teachers seminars for training. However, this solution offers a problem in itself. In February 2009, an article in the Washington Examiner said, "A mandatory training for teachers receiving special needs students into regular classrooms saw little more than 50 percent attendance." The article also said that of the special needs students tested on the Maryland state exam, 100 percent of the students scored at the lowest levels in math and reading.

The best way to learn about a special needs student is to speak with the student's family and ask questions regarding any possibilities that may cause the student distress. If your school district does not offer training or seminars on how to deal with special needs students, look on the Internet and you will find many sites that offer help. One good source is Education World. You can find some resources through them at **www.education-world.com/a_curr/curr139.shtml**.

Building a relationship with your special needs student

You play a key role in building a child's self-esteem and success. By creating a bond with your students with problem behavior or special needs, you are helping ensure their future by instilling self-esteem. You are also helping ensure their best behavior while they are in your care. This practice will also create a better learning environment for all the students under your supervision. Having a good relationship with special needs students is what brings these children competence in school and motivation to participate more in the classroom. It is a fact that students with behavior problems who get along well with their teachers also get along better with their peers and have better social skills. The National Association of School Psychologists (NASP) said "most children pick up positive skills through everyday interactions with adults and peers," and "social skills are linked to the quality of the school environment." NASP enforces the need for students to feel connected and welcomed, saying it is "essential in positive adjustment, self-identification, and developing a sense of trust in others." Feeling safe is critical for a child, especially for their learning and mental health, and it is imperative the school environment give all students a feeling of being safe. When a teacher shows a child that he or she is safe when in their care, this reinforces the availability of adult support. Teaching children social skills in school reinforces positive behavior in all students, and is especially needed in students with behavior problems.

Writer Linda Starr, who works for *Education World*, did research and spoke with several teachers, asking if inclusion really works. The teachers informed Starr that the "social benefits of inclusion provide unexpected educational benefits as well." According to the teachers Starr interviewed, "The normal daily interactions that occur in the classroom allow special education students to form friendships that result in less disruptive behavior, increased independence and self-confidence, and an increased willingness to take academic risks." These teachers also say the regular students became more caring and understanding, and were more willing to give help. In Starr's research, all the students "develop social and academic skills that enhance their classroom achievements."

What few extra hours you may spend learning about your behavior problem or special needs students will be time well-spent. By having a good relationship with these students, you will eliminate the majority of the problems before they take place.

You will never be able to change a child overnight, and you cannot change the problems he or she faces. You can only change how you respond to that child, but that change in response could possibly make all the difference in the world. Once you get to know your student and have changed your response to his or her behavior, you are beginning to inch the student toward trusting you, and it is time to motivate the student to want to succeed.

Behavioral problems are something veteran teacher Jennifer Sherrill understands. She has advice for new teachers that would benefit them to remember.

CASE STUDY: TIPS FROM VETERAN TEACHERS

Jennifer Sherrill
Second-grade teacher
Sunrise Elementary
Palm Bay, Florida

"Each year, I have had a 'problem child' who always ended up being one of my most memorable students," said Sherrill. "The most important thing to do when you get a child who is known for his or her behavior is to take all prior knowledge and realize it should not be the final judgment of the student's behavior." This student may be more mature, more comfortable with you as a teacher, or simply in a better environment at home — all of which can change his or her behavior, she said.

"You will form your own view of the student soon enough, and you do not need someone else's opinion robbing that child of his or her fair chance to make a good first impression. Now, that is not to say that this student will not drive you crazy, but you must remain patient, and you will need to pick your battles," she said.

There will be many things that go on throughout the day where that child will be testing you and you can fail that test or choose to alter it, Sherrill said. "When his or her behavior is stealing the attention of the classroom, try moving his or her desk to the outskirts of the formation. Rather than announcing the bad behavior, try private conversations to help downplay the outburst and direction of attention."

Sherrill once had a student with a behavioral problem who loved toy cars, so she allowed him one toy once a week for good behavior. "Provide an incentive for that student alone," she said. "Positive reinforcement is a necessity for these children; however, do not overdo it, or it will have a negative effect." If this is overdone, the student could come to expect a gift on a regular basis.

To motivate a difficult student, you must plan how you will respond to that student's individual needs. Students with behavior problems believe that all adults will give up on them, and this is why being consistent is so important. Not only do you need to be consistent in your responses, but also in sending a message of caring, hoping, and believing the student can succeed. You want the student to know you believe in him or her, and you hold them to the same expectations as your other students. Doing this will help build a relationship between you and your special needs student and will foster a relationship of trust and respect.

When you understand how a student's life is different from his or her peers' lives, you will have a better understanding of what that student needs.

There are many considerations to take into account to effectively individualize your behavior to that of a problem student, but the three main considerations are:

- Does this student need motivation?
- Is this student in need of limits?
- Does this student act out because of a need for attention?

These three considerations will lead to other questions, but will also lead you to more answers. If the student does not act out because of a need for attention, then why does the student behave this way? You may discover that he or she has a hearing problem and this is what has caused others to think that there is a learning disorder. Once you identify the student's needs, you can better help that student and yourself, as well as the rest of the class. By knowing their needs, you can correct the behavior problem and start encouraging the behavior that should be taking place.

Remember that working with these students will also present an emotional roller coaster for you; be patient and persevere. Do not give up on them, and chances are it will pay off and you will help them succeed — which will make you a successful and more effective teacher.

There are times when a teacher will look at his or her student line-up for the coming year and become excited to find a gifted student on their class roster. If a student is known to be gifted, it will state this in the student's file. What many new teachers are shocked to learn is that sometimes the child who causes the most problems is the gifted student.

The Gifted Student

With gifted students, new teachers usually expect well-mannered, well-behaved students who need little, if any, individual attention, and parents sometimes have the same idea. However, it is not uncommon for gifted students to have a hard time shutting down their inquisitive minds. They are usually the first to take a teacher's lesson far beyond the boundaries of what is being taught.

Gifted students are normally impatient and have a hard time concentrating, sometimes making it difficult to teach them. Because gifted students' abilities are limited in a normal classroom setting, an effective teacher will adjust the content of the lesson to meet the needs of the student. It has been determined that project-based instruction works well for gifted students if they are given a somewhat loose arrangement and allowed to take the assignment as far as they wish. An example of this kind of instruction would be to have the student create a book or a poster on a class subject instead of merely memorizing target words.

Because gifted students become bored and restless, it is a good idea to set a faster pace for their assignments. Because of the freedom to do extensive and fast research, technology also works well for these students and is something a teacher can use to enhance the lesson for the student. With technology, gifted students can do research online. Instead of reading one or two paragraphs on the Civil War, they could use a computer to find, read, and learn many interesting facts that are not written in the history books used in the classroom.

If a gifted student becomes bored, it is not uncommon for them to become disruptive, which is why it is important for teachers to allow gifted students more leeway in a project or lesson than the average student is given.

If a group project is in the works, you should be sure to group the gifted student with other gifted students and some less capable students, which is a good mix to prevent boredom and impatience.

Connecting with a gifted student is sometimes frustrating. The main task will be to keep the student's mind occupied and challenged. This will give the student what he or she needs to be successful in school, and the teacher will not have to worry about disruption. Many times disruption is caused by a student who simply wants to challenge your authority.

The Authority Challengers

The student who holds the attention of his or her peers in your classroom is challenging your authority. This student is certain to make tough, crude remarks at every opportunity, and his or her hostile attitude shows that he or she dares you to do something about it. This student causes disruption in the classroom, which may cause you to feel frustrated and angry. This one student can prevent you from teaching your class, so you want to get control — and you want to do so quickly.

It may be hard to believe, but you are capable of having a dramatic impact on this student. The first step is to gain his or her trust because in this student's eyes, you may be just another adult who should not be trusted. Sometimes these students have parents who are unreliable, inconsistent in parenting, abusive, or too tired and overwhelmed with trying to meet their financial obligations to meet the needs of this child. Due to this kind of neglect, the problem lands in your lap and it is up to you to repair the student's mindset. This is not an easy task, but it is possible.

If you respond negatively to a student who defies you, you will only get more defiance than before. In order to build a relationship and trust with this student, you must first get to know him or her. Understand how that student's world is different from other students' living situations and why. If you consistently show this student you care and take the time to talk with him or her, you will begin to build trust. Be aware that once the trust starts, it is unwise to break it because you will not get another opportunity with this particular student to repair that trust. If the student draws a picture for an assigned project but forgets to title the picture, it would be best to approach the student with detailed praise, saying all the reasons the picture is done very well, then explain, "But you need to title this beautiful picture so it is finished." This way you are giving praise, but also making clear that the title will be the finishing touch to the good work he or she has done.

If you keep humor in your lessons and in your reaction to this student's behavior, he or she will try his or her best not to laugh. Just be careful to never belittle or cause embarrassment to the student. Keep up the humor because eventually you will catch this student enjoying your attempts. Laughter is good for everyone, and even the student with the worst attitude cannot help but get caught up in laughter at some point.

Listening to your students will also impress a child who challenges your authority. These students watch the person they are challenging very carefully, so you will bode well to be sincere and truly care about what your students say and think, which will give the challenger pause in determining whether you are an adult who can be trusted.

Disruption comes and goes in any classroom, but there are times when it is caused by one particular student, and there may be an unsuspected reason behind it.

The Disruptive Student

Many times your disruptive student will suffer from a medical disorder the parents are not aware of. It is not uncommon to find a disruptive student has a mild case of autism, attention deficit disorder (ADD), or attention deficit/hyperactivity disorder (ADHD). These students require more attention than most students, and to be academically successful, they will need the intervention of a special education teacher. The special education teacher will have the student's Individualized Education Plan (IEP), which will contain a general agreement from the team as to what the disability is and the assessed characteristics of the student. This plan will:

- Give a vision of a long-term goal for the student

- Explain the student's disability and how it affects his or her progress in the classroom

- Give a short-term goal based on the student's learning strengths and weaknesses

- Explain how the teacher can accommodate and modify lessons for the student

- Explain how to help the student learn appropriate behavior if the disability can interfere with these skills

The IEP will also give details on summer services, transporting needs, and the best type of placement for the student. It is important to go over the IEP so you can meet the student's needs while he or she is in your class. For these students, you will need to work with the parents as they can give you excellent advice on how to handle certain situations.

An example of this is John, a student who had a mild case of autism. Most of the time John was well-behaved in class, but the teacher did not know that John was terrified of bees. The teacher found out about John's fear when a bee flew in through the open window and John ran from the room screaming. John's parents knew the only way to calm him in such a situation is to remove him from the room until the bee is caught and put outdoors. Unfortunately, the teacher did not know this was the proper way to handle such a situation. After John was calmed and the teacher figured out what had caused his outburst, the problem was immediately taken care of, and precautions were taken to avoid future problems. Parents can tell you trigger points to watch for with a student so that you have a warning of a possible outburst. With this knowledge, you are prepared for a possible incident that you would otherwise have no expectation of.

Disruptive students are sometimes average, special needs, or very smart and simply wanting attention. There may be absolutely nothing wrong with the student other than the need for some guidance or gentle but firm words of encouragement. These students can be very well-behaved and suddenly become extremely disruptive. A good example of this involves two brothers who were students in a special education classroom.

The brothers were very close and grew up looking out for each other. They were good children living in a foster home who had seen more than their share of violence, drugs, and disappointment. When they suddenly began acting out in ways never seen before, the teacher spoke with them and found out that their mother was to appear in court. The boys were hoping she would get out of jail and they could return home. This is an example of why it is imperative to know about the family and environment of your students. Knowing what was happening in the boys' home helped the teacher have more patience and understanding with his students. With a firm but gentle demeanor, the teacher kept the boys under control and gave them the consistency, caring, and nurturing they desperately needed.

A disruptive student sometimes only wants to get into trouble to get attention from his or her parents because the student may think bad attention is better than no attention from his or her parents. Again, getting to know the student and gaining his or her trust is the first step in getting to the root of the problem. Sometimes, getting to know a student can be harder than expected, especially if the student is abnormally stubborn.

The Stubborn Student

Sometimes a stubborn student alone is enough to drive a teacher crazy, especially if the stubborn student is one who can do the work assigned, but refuses. There are also stubborn students who never show whether they can do the work, leaving the teacher in the dark as to what should be assigned. These students are typically regarded as underachievers who may be considered lazy. Even their parents will sometimes label them as such, and the student then labels themselves the same way. They can go through their whole academic life never doing the work and never finding out whether they are truly capable of succeeding. It is quite common for this kind of behavior problem to be caused by an underlying fear of failing.

The gifted student who is stubborn and refuses to try is normally afraid of failing. While you, the student, and the student's parents know the student is capable of doing the work, the student holds a fear of not being able to meet the expectations set for him or her. As a teacher, you will see that the work he or she is handing in is less than what he or she can do, and this can frustrate you. The student senses your frustration and again sees her or himself as failing to meet expectations. It is a vicious circle, and it is best to learn how to deal with this behavior rather than have it repeat itself. The best approach is to start with small expectations on your part and work your way up as the student's trust grows. Ask the student to draw a picture and give praise no matter how little effort is put into it. Give this praise freely while making a suggestion of a small addition the student can put in the picture each time. If the student complies, give even more praise. Working with these students will pay off, but it is a long-term plan that requires patience on the teacher's part.

You can try to motivate the student by making the assignments interesting. The parents can usually tell you what interests them, and this is information you can use. Be aware that it is common for these students to stop trying once they succeed in an assignment, causing more frustration for the teacher and the parents.

These students are overwhelmed easily, thus it is a good idea to offer assistance often. By boosting their self-esteem, you are helping them in more ways than what you may be able to see. It is imperative that you help them with their tasks, show you care, encourage them, assist them when you feel it is needed, praise them, and never let them forget that you care about their future. If you succeed in helping a stubborn student turn his or her life around, you will never forget the experience or the natural high this success gives you. The impact you can have on this student can change his or her future for the better.

Each student is an individual, and even though you must treat them equally, you will learn that you must sometimes put forth a little more effort with some of them. There are some students who need more motivation than others, such as the emotional student.

The Overly Emotional Student

The student who falls into this category is usually a student who needs extra motivation. This student will have a meltdown if pushed to do an assignment that he or she is certain he or she cannot do. Many times a teacher will end up helping this student do the assignment too much and never realize that doing this reinforces the student's belief that he or she is not capable of doing it his or herself.

The first thing you must realize is that, in some cases, this student has absolutely no self-confidence. If you try to help the student do an assignment, you may only be showing that also you have no confidence in the student's ability. By doing the work for him or her, or accepting that the student cannot or will not do the work, you are enabling this student's failure and giving this student what he or she wants — a reason to not do the work.

When you realize you have a student who needs extra motivation, you will have to set goals that will address this need in a more positive way. First, you must assure the student that you believe he or she can do the work. Always have high expectations for the student, letting him or her know he or she is accountable, and you believe he or she is capable.

With these students, you may need to break down the assignment into small parts to help the studenst get started and complete the assignment. With every small part that is finished, whether it is a good job or not, give the students encouragement and praise. Also, if the students are not getting the work done while in the classroom, it must be assigned at another time, such as during recess or library time, again making sure the students know that you have expectations and that they are accountable for getting the work done. This motivates the students to continue doing the work until it is completed.

Every student is an individual, and to be the best teacher possible for them, you must look at each student and decide what he or she needs most to succeed. As a teacher, you will be surrounded by diversity, but rather than see it as a challenge, bask in it and realize how it helps your students learn and grow.

A Diverse Classroom

Because the concept of inclusion means all students should be placed in the least restrictive environment possible, diversity in the classroom has intensified. The argument for inclusion is that students who would be placed in a separate learning environment would not receive the same education as those in a regular classroom. Another perspective of inclusion is that the regular students will view the special needs students as their peers when in the same classroom, limiting prejudice against the special needs children.

The argument against inclusion varies, just as the argument for inclusion varies. One view against inclusion is from parents with disabled children who fear inclusion will mean less attention for their children rather than more attention that they might need. Another argument against full inclusion is it will lead to more prejudice against these students rather than acceptance. Teachers have witnessed students feeling anger because special needs students receive more help and less homework than they did. At the same time, teachers interviewed for *Education World* said almost all regular students have learned more tolerance and patience because of inclusion.

As a teacher, you will be faced with complaints and comments in regard to inclusion from staff, peers, administration, parents, and students. The best defense against this type of conversation is maintaining a positive attitude and treating all your students equally. If you consistently treat your students the same, you will lead by example. However, some situations demand you must take extra time with students who need it, and you will be teaching your students that some people and situations take more patience and help than others.

Every class you have as a teacher will be diverse. You will have students with different abilities, different learning capabilities, dissimilar maturity levels, divergent family situations, and unique backgrounds and ethnicity. These differences will present challenges, but they will also offer a rich experience for you and your students. Veteran teacher Carol Baker said she loves diversity in her classroom: "We can share and learn things about each other. I try to always make sure that we are aware of our differences and celebrate them."

Veteran teacher Jennifer Sherrill thinks teachers should be an example for their students, beginning by embracing the diversity in the classroom.

CASE STUDY: TIPS FROM VETERAN TEACHERS

Jennifer Sherrill
Second-grade teacher
Sunrise Elementary
Palm Bay, Florida

"This year is probably the most diverse class that I have ever had. It is awesome to see how much of a melting pot my room really is. This is just a taste of what I have in my class: students of Hispanic, Korean, and Arabic descent. On the first day of the week, we have 'coffee talk' after our morning work is complete. During this time, the students have seven minutes to share what they did over the weekend. Once the timer goes off, we go back to our chairs, but while they are on the carpet they are one big group of ordinary kids. They get to share stories about what they all have in common, like going to birthday parties, vacations, the park, and so on. It is truly a time to see that no matter how different their skin color or their reading level, deep inside, they are all the same."

Setting an example for your students is something you will find yourself doing daily. It is a constant reminder of how important it is that you be the best person, and the best teacher, you can be. Embracing diversity for your students' benefit is one way you are being the best teacher you can be.

There is diversity all around and it is not just in skin color, eye color, or nationality. There is diversity in individualism. Each year you will look at your roster of new students, and this is the prime time to remind yourself that all of your students deserve the best education you can possibly give them. With an attitude like that, you will be everything your students need you to be.

Effective teachers see the richness of cultural differences in their classrooms and use it for a learning tool. The numerous possibilities for using diversity include tolerance of differences, diversity in foods, and variety in dress, dance, family traditions, and holidays. There are a vast number of lessons with cultural differences in history, languages, weather, seasons, and geography.

Young minds are more open to differences in people, giving them fewer confinements in considering such differences. College professors believe that diversity changes the way students read class material, influences the subjects they choose for research and class projects, and affects how they collaborate in class.

According to research started in 2005 and finished in 2008 by Roslyn Arlin Mickelson with the American Sociological Association's Spivack Program in Applied Social Research and Policy, the effects of desegregated schools and classrooms are positive on achievement and academic success. Diversity improves critical thinking and problem solving skills, and can have positive effects on mathematics and language achievement.

Once again, student success reverts back to the parents, as they have strong influence on how children perceive differences in people. Having a good rapport with the parents is almost as important as having a good rapport with your students.

Maintaining Diplomacy With Parents

Each child and that child's family make one package, and you do not get one without the other. Just as time is a precious commodity to teachers, time is a precious commodity for parents, especially low-income families. Most low-income families cannot afford to miss work, and many of these families work more than one job to stay afloat. It is also common for these families to work odd shifts or irregular hours, making it harder to give time to teachers when asked. These families usually view school and home as two different worlds. They see the teachers as the responsible party for their child's education, and they view their job as a parent to be getting their child to school on time, enforcing the homework policies you set, and teaching their child to behave properly.

It is important that new teachers realize that even families who do not participate in extracurricular activities or school functions still make an essential contribution to the child's development in school and whether that child succeeds. Parents are more likely to become involved in their child's education if they know it will help their child succeed. It is also important that parents believe the teacher is sincere in wanting them to be involved. If they sense the invitation is not sincere, they will never enter the classroom unless they are forced to do so.

Try as you might, you will never be able to please everyone. No matter how hard a teacher tries, there will be times when he or she will have a confrontation with a parent, and sometimes this can be ugly. There are problem parents whether teachers like to admit it or not, and chances are you will meet these types of parents throughout your career. Some of these types of parents include:

- Abusive parents
- Parents with unrealistic expectations
- Parents with addiction problems
- Parents in denial
- Overprotective parents
- Social–ladder obsessed parents

Abusive parents

There are parents who do neglect, abuse, and mistreat their children. This is a fact that, as awful as it is, is something you will most likely have to deal with in your profession. If you see any obvious signs of abuse, such as hand-mark bruising or cigarette burns, immediately report it to your principal and speak with the school counselor. Teachers also need to look for subtle signs of abuse, such as sudden changes in behavior, the student being watchful as though expecting something bad to happen, being overly passive or withdrawn, or coming to school or other school activities early or staying late, and not wanting to go home. Suspicion of abuse must be reported to the social services officers as well. Be aware that this is going to cause hard feelings with the parents, whether the suspicion is confirmed or not, and there will be trust issues with the child as well. If, by chance, the parent comes to the school to confront you, do not under any circumstances get involved in the confrontation. Leave the immediate area and get help, unless it happens to be in your classroom and your students are there.

If that is the case, do not leave your students, but instead send a student to the office to get help if you cannot get the parent to leave the room.

Parents with unrealistic expectations

There are parents who believe their child is a genius or close to it, and if that child does not have the grades they expect, the teacher may be blamed. This is a no-win situation and all a teacher can do is try to assure the parent that the child is giving 100 percent. The best way to assure the parent that the student is doing fine and that the parent may be expecting too much is to have graded papers to show your point to the parent. With these papers you can not only show but explain why you have graded them as you have. A teacher will probably never get through to a parent with this attitude, but will have more work to do to encourage the student. Children who have parents with unrealistic expectations usually have low self-esteem and feel like failures. Giving consistent praise and encouragement is the best antidote for these students.

Parents with addiction problems

The parents with addiction problems are more likely to take out their anger and frustration on you than other parents, whether through a phone call, a note, or during a conference. It is also possible that a child will go home and repeat something learned at school regarding addiction, confronting their parent about the situation. No matter what is said by the parent, it is imperative that you do not argue but remain calm and patient instead. Arguing will only intensify the situation and make problems for you in the long run. It would be wise to speak with your principal and the counselor to discuss what you should or should not say to this type of parent. This not only keeps the principal informed, but also gives you the knowledge of how to deal with these parents. The most important thing you want to stress to a child with addict parents is that the problem his or her parent has is in no way the fault of the student. It is also important to nurture resilience in problem-solving skills and safety planning, such as knowing how to dial 911.

Parents in denial

With these parents, a teacher will spin their wheels and get nowhere. No matter what you say or show them on paper, they will either deny it is true or have a flippant attitude that suggests it is anyone's fault other than their child's. Sometimes a parent may refuse to believe their child has a medical problem such as dyslexia. They may be embarrassed or unable to accept their child is not perfect. The student may have a problem controlling his or her anger, and this too can be hard for a parent to accept. They may not realize there is a problem. It is only right that you take a problem such as stealing, vulgar language, cheating, or hitting another student to the parent and bring it to their attention, but if the parent is one who lives in denial, you may feel it is pointless. The fact is it is the teacher's job to speak with the parent about such behavior, whether it is futile or not. If you cannot get through to the parent, you will have to speak with your principal and school counselor and possibly have a meeting on whether the student needs to be placed in special education classes. Once you have exhausted your means of getting through to the parent, it is time to put the matter into administrative hands.

Overprotective parents

Even though these parents have the best intentions, their overprotective behavior can sometimes make them act irrationally. If a parent calls you and screams about their child crying over having so much homework, listen to what he or she is saying and ignore the screaming. While the screaming may be irrational, there might be a good point somewhere in the flow of words. Irrational behavior can be a refusal to admit the child needs help, be it medical or academic. Parents can be overprotective for various reasons, such as problems in a marriage, or perhaps that parent had inconsiderate parents when he or she was a child. Patience and understanding will get through to these parents faster than anything else, and it is wise to hear them out before interrupting. Let them vent their worries and frustrations, but listen to what they are saying because sometimes there is much to be learned from these parents. Perhaps the parent who is screaming at you about the child crying over too much homework has a good point; maybe you are giving too much homework for the average student. While the parent may be overreacting due to his or her protective nature, there is always a basis for the concern. Remember that parents get very upset when their children are upset, especially if their child is trying their best. Always assure the parent that you realize his or her child is a good student and is trying very hard; inform the parent that you will take their complaint into consideration, then be sure to consider whether their complaint is valid.

Social ladder–obsessed parents

There are some parents who are obsessed with climbing what they see as the top rung of the social ladder, and many times those parents will see the way up that ladder through their child. This is more common in a "sports town" than in other communities; in these areas, academics are not as important as sports. Sometimes the parent is trying to relive his or her life through his or her child, wanting that child to succeed in sports where he or she did not succeed or was forced to give it up. Other times the parent sees the child's success as his or her own; his or her place in the eyes of society is better than another's place, and this kind of parent will incessantly push the child to do better than anyone else. This will cause stress for the student, and when the teacher approaches the parent to speak about the child's academics, the parent will most likely have little to no interest. Be aware that if your school has a policy that the child must carry a certain grade point average to play sports and the child is on the verge of falling below that average, the parent will push the child even harder and may very well take his or her frustration out on you. If it does happen, let your administration know, and inform the parent that his or her child is doing his or her best and you cannot change the rules. If you cannot get through to them, you may have to suggest they take their concern to administration. It is also important to remember that your student is most likely going to be under a lot of stress at home, and this may affect his or her behavior and schoolwork. Be sure to give the student encouragement, and let him or her know that you are there if he or she needs your help with any assignments. By doing this, the student will know you are there if he or she needs you.

Dealing with problem parents requires the same tactics as when dealing with any parents: politeness, respect, courtesy, and professionalism. Try to keep in mind that problem parents may have deep-rooted troubles, usually from their childhood. Compassion will go a long way when dealing with these parents, and you should always maintain a calm demeanor.

There are many problems in the schools, especially public schools, but of all the problems presented, it has been determined that a lack of parent involvement is the leading one. Due to lack of parental concern, some people in society now expect teachers to teach children to have manners, how to be social, and show them how to become adults. Watch the fine line in this expectation, as there are still many parents involved, and some feel this is a line you are not to cross. While you have standards that you expect your students to meet when you develop your lessons, you will have standards to meet that are set by parents. As with your students, parents are individuals, and it will require finesse to deal with each of them in the way that is best. As a professional, you will learn how to do this and become a successful teacher. However, you should always remember that to be a successful teacher, you must also learn to take care of yourself, just as you learn to take care of your students.

Part Four:

Taking Care of You

"I feel [teaching] is the hardest but the most rewarding job there is, other than being a mother or father. Keep everything in perspective, and always do your best. That is all anyone can ask. Don't sweat the small stuff, and pick your battles wisely. You will know you are successful when children remember you and come back to visit or invite you to their graduation party!"

— *Malia Jarvis, kindergarten teacher at Shumaker School in Bellevue, Ohio*

Chapter 10

Preventing Teacher Burnout

Between managing 20 to 30 kids, creating lessons, meeting state and district standards, continuing your education, taking on extra duties, attending mandatory meetings, confronting parents, tackling discipline problems, meeting expectations, dealing with administrative red tape, making evaluations, and dodging disruptions, it is no wonder teachers become stressed. On top of all of these stress factors, teachers also need to find time for a personal life. It is not surprising so many teachers give up the profession and look for a different career. However, if the teachers who quit had known how to reduce their stress, they probably would have stayed with their career choice. As a new teacher, you will have concerns, and it may help to know that all teachers do.

The American Institute of Stress (AIS) reports that the number of employees calling in sick because of stress tripled from 1996 to 2000. This information is based upon teacher information given for the report. They have also reported that being a teacher is the most stressful job in the nation. The stress of being a teacher is reported equivalent or worse than that of a police officer, and is followed by air-traffic controller and medical intern. AIS also states that 40 percent of job turnover is due to stress. In a 2008 study from the University of Kent in England and Martin Luther University in Germany, emotional fatigue from parent interactions and job dissatisfaction superseded all other factors in stress, causing teacher burnout and early retirement.

Stress can cause depression, insomnia, increased blood pressure, rapid heartbeat, a decrease in the immune system, and countless other physical, mental, and emotional ailments. With the list of the teacher's responsibilities growing longer, and the hours to meet those additional responsibilities remaining the same, teachers feel more pressure than ever. The secret to dealing with this insurmountable stress is learning how to survive.

In order to survive the teaching profession, one must first remember that it is a job. This lesson is especially true for new teachers. Teachers are normally tough on themselves because they are nurturers by nature, and this is why they take their job so seriously and will push themselves to the point of getting sick. To prevent this from happening, start a new habit of being easier on yourself. Try to manage your time at school, and when your day is done, leave the job and go home. This is probably the best advice you could possibly take in order to prevent burnout. Veteran teacher Tina Caldarelli knows firsthand about teacher burnout from her experience as a special education instructor.

CASE STUDY: TIPS FROM VETERAN TEACHERS

Tina Caldarelli, Second-grade and emotional support teacher
Cheston Elementary
Easton, Pennsylvania

"The first few years I taught elementary school, I taught special education (emotional support). I had up to four grade levels of students in my room at one time and only one other paraprofessional to assist me. My biggest challenge was trying to teach every child in my class according to their grade level curriculum and their IEP goals. I was pulled in so many different directions. To make it even more difficult, I had to work around the students' special schedules (art, physical education, music, library, etc.) and if they received any special services (such as speech class). It was almost impossible and, most of all, frustrating. Teacher burnout is very common, especially with emotional support and other special education teachers."

Ways to prevent burnout

To keep your professional life and your personal life separate, you must be well-organized and manage your time effectively. There are always papers to grade, classes to take, meetings to attend, and calls to return, so learn to accept this and give yourself time for your personal life. Never allow yourself to think you must have control over every situation; this is an impossible task, and you already have enough to do. Accept that you cannot control every situation you will be faced with in your first year teaching elementary school, but that you can control your feelings and responses.

Here are some tips you can follow to help prevent teaching burnout:

- **Do something for yourself that you enjoy** — Consider going to a festival or a nearby river where you can walk, bike, or run. If you can afford to do so, reserve a hotel room with a hot tub or go camping. Whatever you decide to do, make sure it is something you enjoy.

- **Take up a hobby** — If you take up a hobby, you can share information about what you enjoy doing with your students, or try to incorporate it into one of your lessons during the year. This is also a great way to relax when you are not with your students. If there is something in your past that you have not done in a while, like playing the piano or gardening, consider taking it up again for relaxation.

- **Get plenty of rest** — Sleep deprivation can lead to depression, lack of focus, anxiety, mood swings, and a negative attitude. Lack of sleep over a period of time can cause you to become run-down; your immune system will suffer; and you will become sick, thanks to all the germs your students will expose you to.

- **Exercise** — Not only does exercise allow you to vent frustration, but it also burns negative energy. You could join a gym, take yoga classes, swim, power walk, or run. A bowling league, softball team, or golf course play may be your preference, and any of these are good choices for doing something you enjoy that is good for you mentally and physically. It will also help you keep up with your students while you are at school.

- **Eat healthy meals** — Stress runs down your body, so it is important to eat healthy meals. Sometimes new teachers will get so overwhelmed with the paperwork and grading that they will skip lunch or work so late that the hunger passes. Do not do this to yourself; eating lunch is important for you physically. If you stay after school to get caught up on paperwork, remember to leave at a designated time.

Your health and your personal life are important, too, and if you neglect them, you will be neglecting yourself. This includes your family and friends. Do not swamp yourself with so much work that you forget they are there, and remember that they are also a support system.

The Importance of Family and Friends

When you leave that educational facility for the evening or the weekend, leave it all behind you and turn to the people who are important in your personal life. Veteran teachers Merrisa Herman and Jennifer Sherrill know how important this is.

CASE STUDY: TIPS FROM VETERAN TEACHERS

Merrisa Herman, First-grade teacher
Shumaker Elementary
Bellevue, Ohio

Jennifer Sherrill, Second-grade teacher
Sunrise Elementary
Palm Bay, Florida

"I try to leave my job at school," said Merrisa Herman. "I try not to bring anything home and not think about school when I am spending time with my family and friends. I try to keep a positive attitude and remind myself why I became a teacher: the children."

Jennifer Sherrill described how she copes: "My husband, who is a high school teacher, always reminds me that there has to be a healthy balance between home and school. He is honestly a gauge for me and alters me when I'm too inundated with work and not spending enough time at home or with family. I am so grateful that he keeps me in check because it is all too easy to get immersed with all the little things at work."

Spend time with your family and friends, and remind yourself that they are also a priority. Do not go home night after night and do work, or complain about the day you had. Everyone needs a sounding board, but if you use family and friends for this purpose on a daily basis, you might end up chasing them away.

The reality is no matter how many books you read or how many people you talk to, there will be days that you will be unable to shake off the events that occurred during the job. Perhaps there was a confrontation with a parent, or your principal approached you about a complaint, and the day continuously got worse. These are the days you may need to talk to your spouse or your best friend for a sounding board. This might be the day you enter your home and immediately call your mother to complain about how horrible the day was. It is all right to vent to your family and friends on these days, and they will understand and bee there for you on these occasions.

By doing what is necessary to relieve your stress, you will go into the school the next morning and be the successful, effective teacher your students need. At the same time, you will be taking care of yourself. You will find that having an in-house confidant will also be a great stress reducer.

Finding an In-House Confidant

When your day is stressful because one of your students will not behave, maybe you need to let off a bit of steam. Take a deep breath and try to keep your cool until your lunch break or recess, then find the colleague who has become your friend and let it all out. Chances are he or she will need to do some venting themselves. By talking about your work frustrations with someone whose experiences are similar, you will find encouragement, suggestions, help, probably some humor, and a whole lot of relief. Your colleagues understand your work concerns, your frustrations, your anger, and your annoyances better than anyone else, so allow them to help you through it. It is wise to vent to colleagues, rather than your principal, only because the principal already has so much to do and so many people to listen to. However, if the problem you are having is something that needs the principal's attention and is a matter that needs to be attended to quickly, the principal is the person you should be talking to.

You also might want to consider consulting your mentor for stress relief ideas. Mentors know and understand exactly what you are going through because they have been there. By being able to talk with someone who understands your career, you will feel much better. Many school districts that have a mentor program have a policy that mentors never reveal their private talks with the inductee teachers, keeping their conversations private forever. This protects the mentor as well as the new teachers from being questioned or fired.

Your health and frame of mind is very important not only to you, but to your family, friends, and your students. So find a good friend and take care of yourself, and be sure to return the favor when necessary. Good friends are important, and they help you maintain a positive attitude.

Maintaining a Positive Attitude

Research by psychologist Martin Seligman of the University of Pennsylvania has proved that "optimistic people are happier, healthier, and more successful than those with a negative outlook on life." Everyone falls into a bad mood and becomes negative at some time. It is human nature to react to bad days, but you can stop yourself from doing this by monitoring what you say and think. Attempt to think before you speak, and if you realize you are about to say something negative, stop yourself. If you find yourself feeling depressed, stop and adjust your thoughts. Instead of thinking about things that upset you, start thinking about the things in your life that make you happy; push the negative thoughts out of your mind.

Also smile. Smiling is contagious, as is laughter, and most people around you will respond with the same. Look your colleagues in the eyes and smile, then watch as they smile in return. An environment full of smiling and laughing people is a joyous place to be, for you and for your students.

After implementing all the tips in this chapter and the previous chapters, your first year will be a successful one, but ending the year may be somewhat trying in ways that you do not expect. The end of the year can often be an emotional time.

Chapter 11

Ending the First Year Successfully

Prepare yourself to feel some emotional loss and sadness at the end of the school year, while also feeling relief that the year has finally come to a close. Both of these emotions are perfectly normal, and rest assured they will pass. As a teacher, you will notice that your students may experience the same feelings, and as an effective teacher you will need to help your students feel comfortable expressing these emotions. Not only will the expression of emotions help your students, but it will bring you comfort as well. Some ways you can help your students are:

- **Express your own feelings to your students** — This gives them an influential message that it is all right to express their feelings.

- **Encourage your students to talk about their favorite memories of the year** — This will help you communicate and connect, as well as give you ideas for the following year.

- **Expect some change in the behavior of your students** — Children react to feelings of sadness and loss in different ways.

- **Expect your students to feel anxious about the following year** — Once again, your students know they will eventually be entering new territory and you may want to encourage and assure them that it will be a good change.

- **Help your students keep in touch with one another by sharing contact information.**

- **Have an end-of-the-year party** — This helps you and the students feel some closure.

By helping your students find closure and accept the end of the year, you will be helping yourself do the same. Easing your sadness and accepting the relief as a normal reaction will be an effective way to end your first year as a successful teacher. Another thing you should do as the year comes to an end is reflect upon what all you did during the school year. This will help you gain a better understanding of what worked well in the classroom, as well as what areas you may need to improve upon.

The Significance of Reflection

By reflecting over the past year, you can find situations that you may have wished to handle differently if you had known what to expect or had more experience. At one time or another, everyone wishes he or she had handled something or someone in a different way. By using hindsight, you can plan for a less stressful and more successful year to come.

There are many ways to keep track of your first year to have a clear and objective memory and a comprehensible image of how you want to change things the following year. Some suggestions to keep track of each year's situations, thoughts, ideas, and lessons are:

- **Keep a notebook on your desk so you can jot down thoughts and ideas as they occur.** You can include notes about assignments or lessons that did or did not work well for the students.

- **Video journals are a good way to periodically record yourself while you are teaching.** This will help you see yourself as your students do and will aid you in identifying your strengths and weaknesses.

- **Give your students a questionnaire if age-appropriate, but be sure you do not ask their name to be on the paper.** Ask the students what activities they liked, what they did not, and ask them to give you ideas on what to do next year. The anonymous answers will allow them the freedom of being honest. If the students are too young for a questionnaire, you could ask them what class activity was their favorite, why they enjoyed it, and what they would like to do the following year.

There are a number of questions you can ask yourself to determine whether your first year was successful. If you are honest with yourself, you may find ways to make improvements for the coming year. Some questions you could ask yourself are:

- Do I encourage my students to ask questions?

- Am I providing sufficient time for my students to do their work?

- Does the environment of my classroom encourage the students to participate and take risks on answering questions?

- Do the students see me as a teacher who appreciates and enjoys teaching?

These are some of the questions you could have on your checklist, and you can add to the list as more come to you. With the answers to your questions, you can prepare to make your second year of teaching even more successful than the first. As you reflect over the past year, try to look at yourself objectively. Reflect on your personality, your energy level, and how you did in communicating with students, parents, colleagues, and administration. When you discover your strengths, you can assess how to use them in the classroom the following year. Veteran teachers Jennifer Sherrill, Don Shinton, and Carol Baker agree that reflection is important for effective teachers.

CASE STUDY: TIPS FROM VETERAN TEACHERS

Jennifer Sherrill, Second-grade teacher
Sunrise Elementary
Palm Bay, Florida

Carol Baker, Third-grade teacher
Sunrise Elementary
Palm Bay, Florida

Don Shinton, Fourth-grade teacher
Cheston Elementary
Easton, Pennsylvania

Jennifer Sherrill said efficiency comes from reflection of previous work and the possible adjustments that can be made for improvement. "At the end of the year, I love to make a list of possible changes that I want to make. Throughout the summer, I can put thought into my list so by the time we come back to school, I have a pretty stable idea of what I want to alter," she said.

Throughout the year, you will have ideas about how to improve your classroom materials, lessons, and activities. Use a notebook to write down these ideas so you may find ways to implement them over summer break. Carol Baker used a notebook to jot notes of possible changes: "As the year went on, I had a notepad that I would add to when I did something or thought of something that I would change or make better for the next year. For example, I had things like changing my grading scale, ideas for bulletin boards, and keeping track of events that happen that could possibly come up later with a parent," she said.

Don Shinton said his first year of teaching was hard due to lesson planning. "Since you don't have a toolbox to pull from, you have to be prepared for the unexpected. I spent many hours making sure I was challenging the students in my classroom. It was exhausting," he said. But, Shinton said, "a good teacher should always reflect and adjust to make changes. You will find that no two classes are ever alike, so what worked last year may not work the coming year, or better still when you try something from last year and you make it better."

Remember that self-reflection helps teachers attain expertise and become more effective with each passing year. With reflection, you will collect information regarding classroom events, behaviors of your students, and your own level of satisfaction. Reflection will consistently help you improve your managing and instructional skills.

In their book, *The First Days of School: How to be an Effective Teacher*, authors Harry K. Wong and Rosemary T. Wong wrote, "The professional educator is always learning and growing." When you use reflection for upcoming years, take the time to use the information you gain to set new goals. By implementing your new knowledge, you will find the end result is more time for yourself, your family, and your friends. You will become more organized, allowing more free time and less stress in your life. By using these techniques, you will avoid burnout, enjoy your profession more with each passing year, and be the most effective teacher your students could ever hope for. Becoming an effective teacher is much easier if you speak with the teachers who are successful and learn how they succeeded.

The Secrets of Success

German scientist Georg C. Lichtenberg once said, "One's first step in wisdom is to question everything — and one's last is to come to terms with everything." In your first year, if you want to be an effective elementary teacher, you are going to question everything, including yourself. The best way to prepare for the first year is to heed guidance from those who have already been there, add it with the life experiences you have, and have an abundance of wisdom that will lead you to become the most effective teacher possible.

In talking with experienced teachers, it becomes obvious that the people who become the best teachers are the ones who care about their students — and even they started their first year fearing they would not succeed. When an inexperienced employee is overconfident, it comes across as arrogance, and new teachers are anything but arrogant. Carol Baker said her greatest fear on the first day was that she would not know everything. "In a perfect world, you would leave college with everything you need to be a teacher," she said.

It is common for first-year teachers to be overwhelmed and uncertain, so do not hesitate to ask for help. Veteran teachers will assure you that being fearful is normal, and administration and other teachers are there to help.

Most new teachers are uncertain about their students, and a million questions go through their minds before that first day begins: How will you control your students, manage your classroom, or discipline those who misbehave? These questions are perfectly normal. Veteran teacher Jennifer

Sherrill said her greatest fear was that she would not have any control over the class, and no learning would take place.

"This fear constantly took over until I received my first class. They were a rough bunch, but they wanted to learn. It wasn't long before I knew that I did not need to be fearful," she said.

How can you be successful and still enjoy your job with so many demands placed on you? You can do it by remembering why you decided to teach in the first place.

CASE STUDY: TIPS FROM VETERAN TEACHERS

Jennifer Sherrill, Second-grade teacher
Sunrise Elementary
Palm Bay, Florida

Tina Caldarelli, Second-grade and emotional support teacher
Cheston Elementary
Easton, Pennsylvania

"Teachers are given so many directives and paperwork that take away from what they need to be focusing on in the classroom," said Tina Caldarelli. "I honestly think that teachers need to remind themselves daily that they should do what is best for the students and to enjoy every minute of their opportunity to be such an amazing and influential role model. We constantly lose sight of why we got into teaching in the first place due to all the crazy demands of the administration. There is not as much room for creativity anymore due to intense curriculum guides and new programs constantly being thrown at the teachers. Do this, teach that, you have to do all of it — no exceptions — but there is not enough time in one day to utilize all of the nice kits, etc. We are only one person with a bunch of curious, energetic students, some of whom struggle to get through even just half of the lesson for the day. Do what you can and enjoy it. Then the students will learn and enjoy learning."

As a teacher, you will experience a moment of knowing you are an effective teacher. Jennifer Sherrill said she remembered exactly when she felt as if she was an effective teacher: "Last year (my second year) was full of moments of affirmation for me as a teacher," she said. "As many teachers can relate, your first year is the hardest. However, when those students from your first year come back to visit you before and after school in your second year, it makes you proud of what you did for them. They appreciate you enough to come back and visit over and over and over again. Also, our third-grade team is great about having the students write a thank-you letter to teachers who have made an impact in their lives, and when I went to my mailbox and pulled out a stack of letters, I just stood there and cried as I read them, especially the one from my most challenging student. I still have his letter, and he still visits me to this day. It is moments like that that remind you of how successful you are as a teacher."

Remember, you are going to have trying days, but even those can sometimes turn out to have a silver lining. Fourth-grade teacher Don Shinton told the story of how he had been covering a sixth-grade teacher's classes as a substitute:

"The first day ended with a study hall with fifth graders. I was thankful for that study hall because sixth graders can be merciless to substitute teachers. The second day was equally as challenging. By the end of the day, I had questioned my career change," he said. "If kids were going to be so unappreciative, maybe I had chosen the wrong second career. As I was leaving the building with these thoughts, I heard my name. I could not believe that anyone would know my name after two days. When I turned to see who it was, I was surprised to see the smiling face of a fifth-grade boy who I had helped in the study hall the day before. He said, 'Thanks for your help yesterday.' It was at that point that I realized that I had already made a difference in a child's life, even though I was only a substitute."

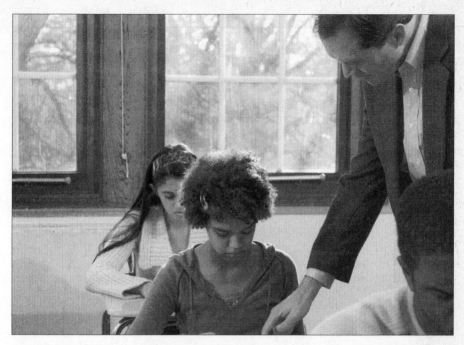

Doris Rayburn is a 35-year veteran teacher in Knoxville, Tennessee. Rayburn has seen many things in her years as an elementary teacher, but her story of how she knew she was a successful teacher is one that will make new teachers realize their value. "One of the first incidents that made me feel successful was during my first year," said Rayburn. "I had a child that wrote upside down and backwards. This was a child who lived in the mountains in Tennessee. Working through social agencies and school personnel, I was able to get him corrective lenses along with other assistance. By the end of the school year, this problem was corrected, and he had mastered most of the first-grade skills."

Make sure you remember that you chose to become a teacher because it is where you wanted to be, and you wanted to be here to make a difference for your students. Knowing how students look at teachers can be a good way to learn how to be more effective. By listening to what they have to say and contemplating how they think of teachers, you will become a better leader and a more effective teacher. When you seriously consider a student's perspective, you will find you are on your way to becoming a successful elementary school teacher.

The Student's Perspective of Teachers

This section of the book will give you more insight and help you understand what students want in their teachers. Asking first or second graders can give you some idea of what they need, but by looking at the way older students view their teachers, you can learn better ways to improve your teaching skills and people skills. This information can give you better ways to communicate and more efficient ways to understand what kids need from the people they spend much of their day with. While it is true younger students may have needs that no longer exist when they become older, students do need many of the same things from their teachers no matter the grade.

The Educational Assessment group of the Pearson and the Quaglia Institute for Student Aspirations released information gathered from the My Voice Aspiration Survey in 2008 that was taken between fall 2006 and spring 2008. The questions were based on opinions about student education, with the answers assessed from 414,000 students within 569 schools in 32 states. The survey discovered 65 percent of the students say their teacher is a positive role model; 48 percent feel their teachers care about them as an individual; and 45 percent feel their teachers care if they do not show up for school.

The Delaware Valley Innovation Network (DVIN), a life science industry that is dedicated to providing the latest information and resources available to foster and grow the tri-state region of Delaware, Pennsylvania, and

New Jersey, has studied what elementary students need from their teachers. DVIN found that the five most important things a teacher can do to most effectively nurture young students are:

- Think long-term by teaching students study skills and how to learn
- Show excitement and enthusiasm
- Communicate with the student and the parents
- Be consistent because students benefit from routine
- Be a role model and tell your students about your own reading and writing experiences

As you can see, for your students to want to learn from you, enthusiasm is essential. If they sense you are bored doing your job, they will be bored with your lessons. To put it in simple terms, if you do not care, they will not care.

Students also want to feel that you care about them as individuals, which is why it is important that you connect with your students and allow them a glimpse into your life. Knowing that you are a person, not just a teacher, will give your students more comfort. This is especially true with young students because it gives them a perspective of you as human, not merely an authority figure.

Making the most of your first year as an elementary teacher will make your profession entertaining, invigorating, and enjoyable. You have chosen a job that most people would not choose to do day after day, making you an invaluable resource for the people of the world. When your students perceive you as an enthusiastic and caring teacher, you have succeeded in your career.

Conclusion

Now that you have a better understanding of what is expected of you and the responsibilities you will have, you should be ready to enter your first year of teaching elementary school. Second only to parents, teachers hold the most enjoyable, important, and influential job in the world.

It is the teachers who encourage and praise our children who are the real heroes in this world — the teachers who give of themselves so freely and make a difference in the future of so many children. As a teacher, you will have the power to improve thousands of lives before your career is over. You are about to embark on a path that you have worked hard for, dreamed of, and sacrificed to get to. Now you have a chance to live that dream while making the lives of thousands of children memorable.

As you enter this world of educating the young and you experience trying days, remember that you are appreciated and respected, and you are a hero or heroine to many children and their parents.

Appendix

Sample Lesson Plans

A good set of lesson plans is vital to ensuring your students are staying engaged in the lesson you are teaching and having an enjoyable experience in your classroom. As you progress through your teaching career, you will make note of which lessons worked especially well, which ones need to be adapted or changed to accommodate your students, and which ones you would never want to try again. Each teacher will approach lesson planning differently, so it may take you some time to figure out which style of planning works best for you. You can make your lessons extremely detailed, including the exact topics and objectives the activity will cover, or you can write a few sentences for each lesson and naturally add information as you progress.

The following plans are ideas you can use during your first year of teaching and beyond. These lessons are tailored to specific holidays and events you will encounter during the school year, and you can adapt them to suit your students' needs as you see fit. There are lesson plans for several different grades included in this Appendix, so every teacher will be able to find an activity his or her class will be able to take part in. *You can also look in the Resources section of this book for Web sites that will offer more ideas for lessons and activities you can plan for your class.*

Lesson 1: First-Day Activity

"All about me" bags

Materials needed:

- Brown paper bags (enough for each student to have one; plan on having extra just in case)

- Pencils

- Crayons

- Markers

- Erasers

- Snack (not necessary for the activity, but all children love a good, healthy snack)

- For older elementary-age students, you can include magazines, scissors, and glue sticks

Begin by writing each student's name on the brown paper bag. When students come into the classroom, tell them to sit at the desk that has the bag with their name on it. Explain to them that this is their "all about me" bag, and they should decorate it with pictures of people or things that are important to them. They can draw family members, friends, pets, activities they like to play — anything they wish to include. You should also participate in this activity so your students can get to know you better.

After enough time has passed (this will vary based on the age of your students, how many other activities you have planned that day, and how detailed you want these bags to be), have each student go around the room and introduce themselves, talking about some of the things on their bags. Make sure you present your bag as well.

At the end of the day, explain to your students that they will need to take home their bags and bring in one item that represents them into the bag. For example, if Blake likes to play baseball with his older brother, he can bring in a baseball. If Melinda likes to dance, she can bring in her ballet shoes. At the beginning of the second day of school, have each student present their items and say what they represent.

Lesson 2: First-Day Activity

Find the gingerbread man

(Use this lesson to get your students better acquainted with where important places are located in your school. This is best for younger students in kindergarten or first grade.)

Materials needed:

- Photos of gingerbread men
- Tape

The day before the first day of school, go around your school's campus and place photos of gingerbread men at all the important locations in your building. Some places you will want to take your students include the main office, restrooms (if there are not any in your classroom), library, cafeteria, nurse's office (if you have one), playground, and any other important location your students may need to visit. You might want to consider placing a gingerbread man where your class is designated to go for a fire drill.

On the first day of school, read your students the story of the Gingerbread Man. Show your students pictures of the Gingerbread Man and explain how he has been hiding in your school. Have your students walk around the school grounds to the different areas where you placed the pictures of the gingerbread men. Make sure when you take your students to each location, they meet an adult whom they will interact with there (for example, meet the librarian at the library). It would be a good idea to let these staff members know your plans on the first day of school so they are prepared to meet your students.

Lesson 3

Open house artwork

(Use this lesson on the day your school schedules Open House night or Back to School night.)

Materials needed:

- A roll of butcher paper
- Markers
- Scissors
- Tape

The day your school has scheduled Open House or Back to School night, tell your students they will be drawing pictures of themselves so their parents can see their desks and the classroom. Have each student lie down on the butcher paper and trace his or her outline. If your students are old enough, have them partner up so they can trace each other on the paper. Use the scissors to cut out each student's outline, making sure to write each student's name above his or her outlined shape.

Have each student draw a likeness of themselves on their piece of paper. Tell them to draw in their eyes, nose, mouth, hair, clothes, and shoes so it looks just like them. After the students are done with their drawings, tape each figure to the back of their chairs (or near where each child sits) so each child's parent or parents can see where the child sits in the room. Not only will this let each child express their creativity, but it will also make your room more lively for when the parents come to visit.

Lesson 4: Halloween

Creating "pumpkin pals"

(This Halloween-themed activity would be good for students in third grade or older.)

Materials needed:

- Construction paper
- Scissors
- Glue
- Markers
- Blank paper
- Pencils
- Yarn
- Buttons
- Any other art supplies you would like to include

Begin this lesson by explaining to students what a biography is. Tell them they will be creating a biography for their very own "pumpkin pal." They should first begin by naming their pumpkin pal, then saying their pal's age, where they live, their likes, and their dislikes. Each student should write these characteristics into a paragraph (or longer, depending on the age of the students).

After each pal's biography is complete, tell your students to draw a picture of what their pumpkin pal looks like. Give your students orange construction paper for the heads, markers, yarn, buttons, glue, or whatever other art supplies you decide to include. After each student has completed the picture of their pal, have them present their pumpkin pal and read each pal's biography aloud to the class. Once the class has finished presenting, hang the pals around the room for decoration.

Lesson 5: Thanksgiving

Turkey hunt

(This lesson is good for students in kindergarten or first grade. Also, the turkeys can be changed for any season of the year: hearts for Valentine's Day, pumpkins for Halloween, or clovers for St. Patrick's Day.)

Materials needed:

- Paper turkey cut-outs (You can make these by tracing your hand on brown paper and coloring the turkeys accordingly, or you can purchase turkey cut-outs.)

- Permanent marker

- Tape

- Rewards (can be stickers or candy)

Make sure you have one turkey cut-out for each student you have in your class. On the back of each turkey, write a number. Make sure that there is only one of each number and that there is tape on the back of the turkeys, so they will stay put when you hide them. While your students are out of the room (at lunchtime or before they arrive for the day), hide the turkeys throughout the classroom. When the students arrive in the classroom, tell them several turkeys have gotten loose and are hidden in the room. Tell your students to each find one turkey, and once they find their bird, to sit down at their desk.

After each student has found a turkey and is seated, have each student say the number that is on the back of their turkey. Ask your class to tell you which of your students has the highest number. The student with the highest number will "win" and may receive a prize; however, make sure all students receive some prize for their participation in the game (you can use stickers or a snack).

HAPPY♥
THANKSGIVING!

Lesson 6: Thanksgiving

Buying a Thanksgiving meal

(This lesson is best suited for third-grade students or older.)

Materials needed:

- Paper

- Pencils

- Play money (optional)

- Calculators

- Grocery circulars from several different grocery stores (You can also make this item if you do not have access to several different stores in your area.)

Tell your students they are going to be responsible for buying all the food for a Thanksgiving dinner for six people. As a whole, ask your class what foods they typically eat at Thanksgiving and write those items on the board. Then divide students up into groups of three or four, depending on the size of your class. Give each group $100 to use when planning their meal (this is where the optional play money comes in) and give them a calculator. They will also need paper and pencil to keep track of the food items they are buying. Provide each group with a grocery store circular so they know how much each food item will cost (you can have them round up to the nearest dollar or create your own circular so you can create prices for the food items).

Have each group work together and purchase all the food they will need for their Thanksgiving dinners. After about 15 to 20 minutes, have the groups get back together and write their grocery lists on the board. Add up how much each group spent, and compare how much of each food item all the groups purchased. You can create a bar graph to display which Thanksgiving items were the most popular among your classroom.

Lesson 7: Winter Holidays

Making marshmallow snowmen

(This lesson is best for students in kindergarten or first grade.)

Materials needed:

- Jumbo marshmallows (enough for each student to have two and additional ones for them to eat)

- Toothpicks (optional)

- Markers

Pass out two marshmallows for each student. Have them stack the marshmallows on top of each other. The students can either lick the marshmallows and stick them to each other or press a toothpick through the marshmallows to keep them together. After the marshmallows are stuck together, have students draw faces and buttons on their snowmen.

Allow students to enjoy eating the extra marshmallows, but make sure they know not to eat the marshmallows they colored.

Lesson 8: Winter Holidays

Why the Grinch should love Christmas

(This activity is best suited for children in first to third grade.)

Materials needed:

- A copy of either the movie or the book *How the Grinch Stole Christmas*

- A drawing of the Grinch or an inexpensive stuffed Grinch

- A notebook for the Grinch's journal

- Paper

- Pencils

Either read or watch *How the Grinch Stole Christmas* with your students. The following day, write a letter from the Grinch explaining why he hates Christmas. Have each of your students write the Grinch a letter explaining why Christmas is such a good holiday and why they enjoy it so much. Invite students to tell the Grinch about the best Christmas they ever had. Ask a few students each day to read their letter to the Grinch out loud for the class.

Do this activity every day with a different letter from the Grinch. Make sure the letter from the Grinch gives a different reason for why he dislikes the holiday. For example, one day the Grinch could hate Christmas because it is in winter and he hates the snow. Your letter to the Grinch could explain how much you love snow around the holidays because you can make snow angels, go sledding, make snowmen, and have snowball fights with your family.

Lesson 9: Black History Month

Walking through history

(This lesson is best suited for fourth- or fifth-grade students.)

Materials needed:

- Access to encyclopedias, library books, or the Internet
- Paper
- Pencils

Compile a list of African-American leaders who have made significant contributions to American life, making sure there is one African-American listed for each student in your class. Write the names of each African-American on a slip of paper and have your students pull a piece of paper out of a hat or bag. Tell students they will need to write two or three paragraphs about the leader they selected. Inform students that while they are researching their leader they will need to answer the question, "What did they contribute to society?"

After students have written about their leaders, have them construct a monument in honor of that person. For example, if a student selected Thurgood Marshall, he or she could construct a monument of a gavel to commemorate the fact he was the first African-American to serve on the Supreme Court. Or if he or she picked the name Rosa Parks, he or she could bring in a school bus made from a shoe box.

Ask student to bring in the monuments and descriptions of their leaders and place them around the room. Have your students walk around the classroom, examining all the monuments and giving them time to read each leader's description of what they contributed to American society.

Lesson 10: Valentine's Day

Graphing Valentine's Day hearts

(This lesson would be best for second- through fourth-grade students.)

Materials needed:

- Pieces of graph paper (plain or lined paper would also work)
- Pencils
- Boxes of candy hearts, one small box for each student

Pass out a box of candy hearts for each of your students. Ask each student to look at the box of candy (without opening it) and guess the number of pink hearts in the box. Ask them to write down their guess for how many there are in their box. Then ask them how many white hearts there are, and then how many purple hearts. Repeat this step until students have guessed how many of each color there are in their box and have written down all their guesses.

After you have gone through all the colors in the boxes, tell students to open up the candy boxes and divide up the candy by color. Make sure you tell them not to eat any of the candy. Have them draw a basic bar graph, with each bar representing the color of one of the hearts. Once the students have finished drawing their bar graphs, place the graphs on the board so they can see how many of each colored candy the other students had. After this lesson is complete, the students can eat their candy hearts.

Lesson 11: Valentine's Day

Famous pairs game

(This game is best for students in third grade or older.)

Materials needed:

- Two copies of the pairing list that follows
- Scissors
- A hat or bag to place pieces of paper into

For this activity, create two copies of the list of pairings. The first list should be the answer sheet you will use as a reference. For the second sheet, cut the pair in half so there are slips of paper for each word in pairing. Place these slips of paper in a hat or bag, and have each child go around the room and draw a slip of paper. For example, if the child draws the word "macaroni," have the other children around the room raise their hand if they know the correct word that is paired with the word that has been drawn (in this case, "cheese" is the correct answer). The child whom you call on with the correct answer will be the next to draw.

This game can continue for as long as you would like, and you can create your own pairings to include. Some of the pairings suggested for this game are as follows:

Peanut butter and jelly	Black and white
Cat and mouse	Cookies and milk
Coloring book ad crayons	Coat and tie
Hamburger and fries	Jack and Jill
Hugs and kisses	Salt and pepper

Reading and writing	Sticks and stones
Bat and ball	Thunder and lightning
Pencil and paper	Burt and Ernie
Bread and butter	Bees and honey
Table and chair	Bow and arrow
Barbie and Ken	Batman and Robin
Chips and dip	Cake and ice cream
Macaroni and cheese	Shoes and socks
Shirt and pants	Spaghetti and meatballs
Desk and chair	Hammer and nail
Washer and dryer	Pots and pans
Toothbrush and toothpaste	Sugar and spice

Resources

Lesson Plans, Activities, Software, Games, Worksheets, and More

EdHelper (**www.edHelper.com**) — EdHelper is an online subscription service that provides printable worksheets for teachers and parents. EdHelper offers a range of materials including math papers, language arts worksheets, reading and writing assignments, social studies papers, science exercises, and more.

Boardgames.com (**www.boardgames.com**) — Here you will find electronic, handheld, and traditional board games for your students.

Out of the Box Games (**www.otb-games.com**) — An assortment of games can be found here, including dice games, word games, and card games.

Edutopia (**www.edutopia.org**) — Edutopia offers practical advice, lively contributions from teachers, and invaluable tips and tools.

Speakaboos (**www.speakaboos.com/teachers**) — Speakaboos has classic children's entertainment put into a digital world. Speakaboos' stories fall into five genres: fables, fairy tales, folk tales, nursery rhymes, and lullabies. You can find story guides, worksheets, arts and crafts, and more to help your students improve their reading, listening, writing, and computer skills.

Education.com (www.education.com) — Here you will find access to thousands of articles. You may print hundreds of activities that are sorted by grade level and topic. You can also find support and share advice with other teachers, and have access to online tutoring services. There are math programs, educational games, and online reading programs.

Dover Publications (http://store.doverpublications.com) — Find free book samples for education at this Web site. The Dovers have been in business for about 60 years, and their reputation for educational books is immaculate.

ABC Teach (www.abcteach.com) — This is a user-friendly educational Web site that provides printable materials for teachers and parents.

School Express (www.schoolexpress.com) — This site offers educational materials, including more than 16,000 worksheets, activities, games, and software.

Disney Family Fun (http://familyfun.com) — This site offers freebies, including crafts, games, puzzles, holiday ideas, recipes, and more. There is also a magazine available.

Pro Teacher (www.proteacher.com) — This Web site offers just about everything a teacher needs. Here you can find support and networking for teachers as well as materials for reading and language arts.

A to Z Teacher Stuff (**www.atozteacherstuff.com**) — This Web site was created by teachers and has lesson plans, thematic units, teacher tips, and discussion forums for teachers. You can also find downloadable teaching materials and eBooks, as well as printable worksheets, emergent reader books, themes, and more.

Academic Software (**www.academicsoftwareusa.com**) — This resource has educational software, computer supplies, and related products. There is also a staff to help you find the right educational program for your students.

Educational Clip Art (**www.school-clip-art.com**) — This site offers humorous clip art images that you can use on your worksheets to motivate your students. It also offers a link to coloring pages that you can print out for free. This is a good resource for that filler work you may want your substitute teacher to have on hand.

Certificate Maker (**www.certificatemaker.com**) — Here you will find easy-to-use templates for making certificates that you can use to give your students as praise for good work.

Edu Hound (**www.eduhound.com**) — A score of resources can be found at Edu Hound for teachers K-12, including clip art and topic-based online education resources.

Professional Development

Pearson's Online Professional Development (**www.pearsoned.com/ pr_2009/042109.htm**) — Pearson offers product-based tutorials and live Webinars for professional development and training. These are for kindergarten through high school teachers.

Coalition of Essential Schools (www.essentialschools.org) — This coalition provides professional development and networking opportunities for teachers.

National Board for Professional Teaching Standards (www.nbpts.org) — This organization's purpose is to improve the quality of teaching. They do this by developing professional standards and a voluntary system to certify teachers.

National Education Association (www.nea.org) — The NEA is the largest organization in the United States for educators and boasts more than 3.2 million members.

Bulletin Board Ideas

The Teacher's Corner (www.theteacherscorner.net/bulletinboards) — You will find seasonal ideas as well as ideas of general interest at this Web site.

Kathy Schrock's Guide for Educators (http://school.discovery.com/schrockguide) — When you enter the home page of this site, you will need to type "bulletin board" into the search area. You will find dozens of links for bulletin board ideas.

Kim's Korner (www.kimskorner4teachertalk.com) — This Web site is managed by teacher Kim Steele. The bulletin board section gives information about topics for bulletin boards, bulletin board trims, and inexpensive materials. There are also numerous links to other sites.

Electronic Grade Books

Some schools require all teachers use an electronic grade book, and some school districts also require the same electronic grade program. If this is true in your school district, be sure to save your grades in several places, especially on paper. Also be sure to keep them in a secure place.

Learner Profile (www.learnerprofile.com) — This grade book records grades and also tracks yearly progress.

GradeBookWizard (www.gradebookwizard.com) — On this site, you can access your students' grades and attendance information.

Interview Questions for Teaching Jobs

Lesley University Career Resource Center (www.lesley.edu/services/crc/interviewforteachers.html) — This site is intended for teachers, school counselors, and specialists. Created by the Career Resource Center at Lesley University in Cambridge, Massachusetts, this site breaks down interview questions into the following categories: general questions, questions about student teaching, questions for elementary teachers, questions for teachers K-12, questions for special education teachers, questions for school counselors, types of interview questions, and questions to ask the interviewer.

Teaching Interview (www.teachinginterview.com/teacherinterview-questions.html) — This Web site is a guide for landing a teaching job. There are 100 questions listed that are asked at teaching interviews all the time, as well as an eBook, articles on teacher portfolios, and teaching interview tips.

A+ Resumes for Teachers (http://resumes-for-teachers.com/news/education-interview-questions.htm) — Candace Davies, a global career management professional, is dedicated to assisting teachers. On this site you will find résumé and cover letter samples, interview questions, and free job search help.

American Association for Employment in Education (www.aaee.org/cwt/external/wcpages/links) — In order to have access to all the resources available on this Web site, you must be a member. However, if you click on the "helpful links" section on the left side of the home page, you will connect to a list of helpful links that covers everything from navigating the teacher job market to the basics to teacher preparation by state and field.

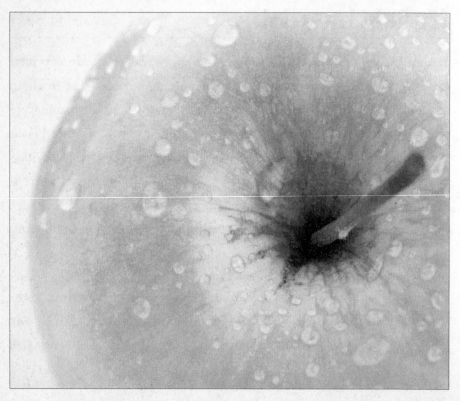

Bibliography

AbsoluteAstronomy.com, "Education in the United States," <**www.abso-luteastronomy.com/topics/Education_in_the_United_States**> Accessed September 1, 2009.

American Council on Education and American Association of University Professors, "Does Diversity Make a Difference? Three Research Studies on Diversity in College Classrooms" 2000 <**www.acenet.edu/bookstore/pdf/diversity_report/2000_diversity_summary.pdf**> Accessed January 15, 2010.

American Institute of Stress, "Job Stress," <**www.stress.org/job.htm?AIS=e14896988f2f2cc7e1e80144212cfbe3**> Accessed August 24, 2009.

American School Directory, "Providing K-12 School Information," 2009, <**www. asd.com**> Accessed January 1, 2010.

Anxiety Disorders Association of America, "So Your Child Doesn't Want to go to School," 2009, <**www.adaa.org/aboutADAA/newsletter/Schoo-lAnxiety.htm**> Accessed May 20, 2009.

Armentor, Elizabeth, "The Online Teacher's Workload — What to Expect and How to Handle It," 2009, <**www.world widelearn.com/teachers-aid/ article/the-online-teachers-workload.htm**> Accessed June 20, 2009.

Associated Press, "Principal Fired for Refusal to Take More Students," 25 August 2006, <**www.msnbc.msn.com/id/14516170/from/RSS**> Accessed July 17, 2009.

Bochan, Toby Leah, "Wrapping Up the School Year," 2009, Scholastic, <**www2.scholastic.com/browse/article.jsp?id=1433**> Accessed August 17, 2009.

Brevard County Public Schools Professional Development, "Brevard County Induction Program," 2002, <**http://professionaldevelopment. brevard.k12.fl.us/documents/induction/induction%20overview.pdf**> Accessed July 19, 2009.

Brewster, Cori and Railsback, Jennifer, "Supporting Beginning Teachers: How Administrators, Teachers and Policymakers Can Help New Teachers Succeed," May 2001, Northwest Regional Educational Library, <**www. nwrel.org/request/may01**> Accessed May 19, 2009.

Brophy, Jere, "Working with Shy or Withdrawn Students," 1996, ERIC Digest, <**www.ericdigests.org/1997-3/shy.html**> Accessed July 22, 2009.

California State Lottery, "Lottery Funds at Work: Where Does All the Money Go?" 8 May 2009, Calottery.com, <**www.calottery.com/support/ lotteryfunds**> Accessed July 17, 2009.

Canter, Lee and Canter, Marlene, *Assertive Discipline*, Bloomington, IN: Solution Tree, 2001.

Canter, Lee and Canter, Marlene, *Parents on Your Side*, Santa Monica: Lee Canter and Associates, 1991.

Canter, Lee and Canter, Marlene, *Succeeding With Difficult Students*, Bloomington, Solution Tree, 1993.

Canter, Lee and Hausner, Lee, *Homework Without Tears*, New York: Perennial, 1987.

Cavanaugh, Terrence W., "Preparing Teachers for the Inclusion Classroom: Understanding Assistive Technology and its Role in Education," University of North Florida, <**www.unf.edu/~tcavanau/presentations/preparing_teachers_for_the_inclu.htm**> Accessed June 30, 2009.

Center for Excellence in Teaching and Learning, "Never Stop Trying," 2005-2009, Minnesota State University Mankato, <**www.mnsu.edu/cetl/teachingresources/articles**> Accessed May 21, 2009.

Class Size Matters, "The Benefits of Smaller Classes: What the Research Shows," Class Size Matters Online, November 2008, <**www.classsizematters.org/benefits.html**> Accessed September 4, 2009.

Columbia University Record, "Report Finds Overcrowding in New York City Schools at Crisis Level," 17 February 1995, <**www.columbia.edu/cu/record/archives/vol20/vol20_iss17/record2017.31.html**> Accessed July 18, 2009.

Corcoran, Thomas B., "Helping Teachers Teach Well: Transforming Professional Development," June 1995, Consortium for Policy Research in Education, <**www.ed.gov/pubs/CPRE/t61/index.html**> Accessed January 1, 2010.

Cuper, Prudence H. and Stone, Randi, *Best Practices for Teacher Leadership: What Award-Winning Teachers Do for Their Professional Learning Communities*, Thousand Oaks, California: Corwin Press, 2006.

Diamond, Sarah, "Teachers in Distress," 2007, <**http://teachersindistress. com**> Accessed May 21, 2009.

Doolittle, Peter, "Teacher Portfolio Assessment," 2000, <**http://searcheric. org/digests/ed385608. html**> Accessed May 21, 2009.

Durham University's Curriculum, Evaluation, and Management Centre, "Reception Year Teachers Most Important for Primary Education," The Medical News, September 2007. <**www.news-medical.net/ news/2007/09/10/29608.aspx**> Accessed May 6, 2009.

EarnMyDegree.com, "Elementary Schoolteachers , Except Special Education," 2003-2009, <**www.earnmydegree.com/online-education/careers/ education-training-and-library/elementary-school-teachers-except-special-education.html**> Accessed May 20, 2009.

EdSource, "Students with Special Needs," 2009, <**www.edsource.org/ iss_fedlaws_ specialed.html**> Accessed June 30, 2009.

Geisinger, Kurt F. and Carlson, Janet F., "Assessing Language-Minority Students," 1992, <**http://pareonline.net/getvn.asp?v=3&n=2**> Accessed January 15, 2010.

Hassett, Marie F., "What Makes a Good Teacher," System for Adult Basic Education Support, Winter 2000 <**www.sabes.org/resources/publications/adventures/vol12/12hassett.htm**> Accessed May 7, 2009.

Hershman, Dyan M. and McDonald, Emma S., *Survival Kit for New Teachers*, Dallas: Inspiring Teachers Publishing, Inc., 1998.

Higher Education for Development, "Basic Kindergarten Teacher Training Manual," 2005, <**www.hedprogram.org/Portals/0/PDFs/ECE%20 Framework%20Manuals.pdf**> Accessed May 21, 2009.

Hot Chalk's LessonPlansPage.com, <**www.lessonplanspage.com**> Accessed January 27, 2010.

Kaiser, Barbara and Rasminsky, Judy Sklar, *Challenging Behavior in Elementary and Middle School*, Upper Saddle River, New Jersey: Pearson, 2009.

Keeney, Carol, *Brand New Teacher*, Monroe, Connecticut: Vested Publishing, 2006.

Kelly, Melissa, *The Everything New Teacher Book*, Avon, Massachusetts: Adams Media Corporation, 2004.

Kelly, Melissa, "How Budget Cuts Affect Teachers," 2009, About.com, <**http://712educators.about.com/od/issuesineducation/tp/teaching_ budget_cuts.htm**> Accessed July 17, 2009.

Kelly, Melissa, "Teaching at Private vs. Public Schools," 2009, About.com, <**http://712educators.about.com/od/jobopenings/a/private-public. htm**> Accessed June 22, 2009.

Kelley, Michael W., *Rookie Teaching for Dummies*, New York: Wiley Publishing, 2003.

Kolodner, Meredith, "New York City Schools Suffer Massive Overcrowding, Statistics Show," NewYorkDailyNews.com, 2 October 2008, <**www.nydailynews.com/ny_local/education/2008/10/02/2008-10-02_new_york_city_schools_suffer_massive_ove.html**> Accessed September 4, 2009.

Kowal, Julie, Hassel, Emily Ayscue, and Hassel, Bryan C., "Teacher Compensation in Charter and Private Schools," 2008, Center for American Progress,   <**www.americanprogress.org/issues/2007/02/pdf/teacher_compensation.pdf**> Accessed September 2, 2009.

Lawler, Ellen M., Chen, X. Mara, and Venso, Elichia A., "Student Perspectives on Teaching Techniques and Outstanding Teachers," October 2007, <**www.iupui.edu/~josotl/ VOL_7/No_2/v7n2lawler.pdf**> Accessed September 5, 2009.

Learning Rx Center, "Special Education Costs," Learning Rx Inc., 2009, <**www.learning rx.com/special-education-costs-faq.htm**> Accessed September 2, 2009.

Leigh, Andrew and Mead, Sarah, "Lifting Teacher Performance," 19 April 2005, <**www.ppionline.org/ppi_ci.cfm?knlgAreaID=110&subsecid=135&contentid=253286**> Accessed May 21, 2009.

Lesley University, "Interview Questions for Educators," 19 January 2007, <**www.lesley.edu/services/crc/interviewforteachers.html**> Accessed September 5, 2009.

Levin, Jessica, Mulhern, Jennifer, and Schunck, Joan, "Unintended Consequences: The Case for Staffing Rules in Urban Teachers Union Contracts," 2005, The New Teacher Project, <**www.tntp.org/files/UnintendedConsequences.pdf**> Accessed May 21, 2009.

Lopez, Janet Kier, "Funds of Knowledge," 2008, <**www.learnnc.org/lp/pages/939**> Accessed July 20, 2009.

Markway, Barbara D. and Markway, Gregory, *Painfully Shy: How to Overcome Social Anxiety and Reclaim Your Life* New York: St. Martin's Griffin/Thomas Dunne Books, 2003.

McGrady, Sean, "Do Teachers Make A's?" Knight Rider, 5 November 2008, <**www2.nr.edu/kr/?p=105**> Accessed September 5, 2009.

McKay, Dawn Rosenberg "Teacher: Career Information," 2008, About.com, <**http://careerplanning.about.com/od/occupations/p/teacher.htm**> Accessed May 20, 2009.

Mehta, Seema, "Santa Ana's Class Size Woes Expand," 25 July 2007, Los Angeles Times, <**http://articles.latimes.com/2007/jul/25/local/me-santaana25**> Accessed July 18, 2009.

Messina, James J., "Federal Laws Governing Education For Exceptional Students," 2008, <**www.livestrong.com/article/14755-federal-laws-governing-education-for-exceptional-students**> Accessed March 4, 2008.

Michigan Department of Education, "What Research Says about Parent Involvement in Children's Education," March 2002, <**www.michigan.gov/documents/Final_Parent_Involvement_Fact_Sheet_14732_7.pdf**> Accessed December 30, 2009.

Miller, Raegen and Chait, Robin, "Teachers Turnover, Tenure Policies, and the Distribution of Teacher Quality," December 2008, Center for American Progress, <**www.americanprogress.org/issues/2008/12/pdf/ teacher_attrition.pdf**> Accessed September 2, 2009.

Montana State University Billings, "Interview Questions for Teachers," 2009, <**www.msubillings.edu/careers/teacher%20interview.htm**> Accessed September 5, 2009.

Nagem, Sarah, "Students, Teachers Say Goodbye for Summer," 11 June 2008, SalisburyPost.com <**www.salisburypost.com/Area/061108-stu- dents-teachers-say-goodbye**> Accessed August 17, 2009.

National Association for the Education of Young Children, "Helping Young Children Start School," 2008, <**www.naeyc.org/ece/2005/08.asp**> Accessed May 7, 2009.

National Association for Year Round Education, "Typical Year-Round Cal- endars" 2007, <**www.nayre.org/cal.htm**> Accessed August 15, 2009.

National Association of School Psychologists, "Social Skills: Promoting Positive Behavior, Academic Success, and School Safety," 2002, <**www. nasponline.org/resources/factsheets/socialskills_fs.aspx**> Accessed December 28, 2009.

National Center for Alternative Certification, "Alternative Routes to Teacher Certification: An Overview," 2006, <**www.teach-now.org/over- view.html**> Accessed August 17, 2009.

National Center for Education Statistics, "Fast Facts: Are There Any Back to School Statistics for 2009?" 2009, <**http://nces.ed.gov/fastfacts/display.asp?id=372**> Accessed September 5, 2009.

National Council for Accreditation of Teacher Education, "Making a Difference," 1 July 2009, <**www.ncate.org/public/aboutNCATE.asp**> Accessed January 2, 2010.

Neighborhood Capital Budget Group, "National Crisis," 2001, <**www.ncbg.org/schools/national_crisis.htm**> Accessed July 18, 2009.

Pearson Education, "What Students Think: Pearson Announces Results of Largest National Student Survey," 13 November 2008, <**www.pearsoned.com/pr_2008/111308.htm**> Accessed September 1, 2009.

Petkus, Thadra, "Teachers Plan Ahead for New School Year," 22 July 2009, Suite101.com, <**http://curriculalessons.suite101.com/article.cfm/teachers_plan_ahead_for_new_school_year**> Accessed August 17, 2009.

"Political Socialization: Molding Political Ideology One Step at a Time," 4 January 2009, <**http://socyberty.com/politics/political-socialization-molding-political-ideology-one-step-at-a-time**> Accessed August 14, 2009.

Princeton University, "Teaching New Skills to Teachers," <**www.princeton.edu/~edutech/training/tra_level_1.html**> Accessed May 21, 2009.

PsychSite, "Student Perspectives on Good Teaching," <**www.abacon.com/psychsite/toolbox5.html**> Accessed May 21, 2009.

The Regents of the University of Michigan, "Inner-City Schooling: How Do Inner-City Schools Affect Student Achievement?" 2009, <**http://sitemaker.umich.edu/mitchellyellin.356/home**> Accessed July 20, 2009.

Reese, Ruth, "Teacher Stress: The Search for Accurate View and Remedies that Work," 2003, <**www.hicsocial.org/Social2003Proceedings/Ruth%20Reese.pdf**> Accessed May 21, 2009.

Reis, Richard M., "What Makes a Good Teacher Article," Minnesota State University Mankato. 2005-2009 <**www.mnsu.edu/cetl/teachingresources/articles/goodteacher.html**> Accessed May 6, 2009.

Ricker, Marlene, "Inner-City Schools; How to Keep the Elite," 2005, <**http://main.uab.edu/show.asp?durki=91334**>   Accessed   June 20, 2009.

Rominger, Lynne, Heisinger, Karen, and Elkin, Natalie, *Your First Year as an Elementary School Teacher*, New York: Three Rivers Press, 2001.

Sasson, Dorit, "The Organized Teacher and Mentor," 3 June 2007, Suite101.com,   <**http://teacher-mentorship.suite101.com/article.cfm/the_organized_teacher_mentor**> Accessed July 19, 2009.

Shurcliff, Meggie, "Do Mothers or Fathers Influence Children's Political Views More?" <**www.bbn-school.org/us/math/ap_stats/project_abstracts_folder/proj_student_research_folder/children_shurcliff/childs_politics_shurcliff.htm**> Accessed September 1, 2009.

Siddiqui, Owais, "Teacher's Stress 75," 2009, <**http://hubpages.com/hub/Teachers-Stress**> Accessed May 21, 2009.

The Sloan Consortium, "Making the Grade: Online Education in the United States, 2006," 2008 <**www.sloan-c.org/publications/survey/survey06.asp**> Accessed June 20, 2009.

Smith, Charles, A., "Dealing With Sadness and Loss," 1992, National Network for Child Care, <**www.nncc.org/Guidance/dc15_deal.sad.loss.html**> Accessed August 17, 2009.

Star, Linda, "Does Inclusion Help or Hurt Students?" 2009, Education World, <**www.educationworld.com/a_issues/issues240.shtml**> Accessed January 15, 2010.

Stasz, Cathleen, Krop, Cathy, Rastegar, Afshin, and Vuollo, Mirka, "The Step by Step Early Childhood Education Program: Assessment of Reach and Sustainability," 2008, Rand Corporation, <**www.rand.org/pubs/technical_reports/2008/RAND_TR593.sum.pdf**> Accessed May 21, 2009.

Stoudt, Alisa, "*Separation Anxiety 101*," 2009, Education.com, <**www.education.com/magazine/article/separation-anxiety-101**> Accessed July 22, 2009.

Sullivan, Elizabeth, and Keeney, Elizabeth, "Teachers Talk: School Culture, Safety and Human Rights," Fall 2008, National Economic and Social Rights Initiative, <**www.nesri.org/Teachers_Talk.pdf**> Accessed July 18, 2009.

Taylor, Catherine, "What is a Good Teacher?" May 1998, <**www.kyrene.k12.az.us/kea/pdf/MembersSpeaktarticles/goodteach.pdf**> Accessed May 21, 2009.

"Teacher Reflection," 17 February 2008, <**http://calteacherblog.blog-spot.com/2008/02/teacher-reflection.html**> Accessed August 17, 2009.

"Teachers, Tenure, and Poor Quality," AZFamily.com, 11 March 2008, <**www.azfamily.com/forums/viewtopic.php?t=25653**> Accessed May 21, 2009.

TeachNet.com, "Teacher Self-Reflection Checklist-English," 2009, <**www.teachnet.com/how-to/organization/092998.html**> Accessed August 17, 2009.

Thompson, Julia G., *The First-Year Teacher's Survival Guide*, San Francisco: Jossey-Bass, 2007.

"Top 10 Virtual (Work From Home) Careers for 2008," Capital Creative Inc.,   <**www.scribd.com/doc/916383/Top-Ten-Virtual-Work-from-Home-Careers-for-2008**>, Accessed September 1, 2009.

United Nations International Children's Emergency Fund, "Quality Primary Education: The Potential to Transform Society in a Single Generation." <**www.unicef.org/dprk/qpe.pdf**> Accessed June 12, 2009.

U.S. Charter Schools, "About the Charter School Movement," 2000, <**www.uscharterschools.org/pub/uscs_docs/o/movement.htm**> Accessed June 20, 2009.

U.S. Department of Labor Bureau of Labor Statistics, "Occupational Outlook Handbook, 2008-09 Edition" 2008-2009, <**http://stats.bls.gov/oco/ocos069.htm**> Accessed May 20, 2009.

Wagaman, Jennifer, "How to Work with a Student Teacher: Providing Great Teacher Training in Your Classroom," 12 December 2008, About. com, <**http://newteachersupport.suite101.com/article.cfm/how_to_ work_with_a_student_teacher**> Accessed May 21, 2009.

Wagaman, Jennifer, "Support for New Teachers: The Importance of Teacher Mentorship Programs," 26 January 2009, About.com, <**http:// teachermentorship.suite101.com/article.cfm/new_teacher_support**> Accessed July 8, 2009.

Warner, Jack, Bryan, Clyde, and Warner, Diane, *The Unauthorized Teacher's Survival Guide*, Indianapolis, JIST Publishing, 2006.

WFTV.com, "Students, Teachers, Protest School Budget Cuts," 2009, <**www.wftv.com/news/18809269/detail.html**> Accessed August 15, 2009.

Wong, Harry K. and Wong, Rosemary T., *How to be an Effective Teacher The First Days of School*, Mountain View, California: Harry K. Wong Publications, Inc., 2005.

The White House, "Education: Progress," 2009, <**www.whitehouse.gov/ issues/education**> Accessed June 30, 2009.

Young, Bob, "Alums, Teachers Say Goodbye to Summit K-12," 2009, Seattle Times, <**http://seattletimes.nwsource.com/html/education/2009282100_summit31m.html**> Accessed August 14, 2009.

"100 Teacher Interview Questions That Are Asked All the Time," 2008. <**www.teachinginterview.com/teacherinterviewquestions.html**> Accessed September 5, 2009.

Author Biography

With insightful encouragement from her sixth-grade teacher, Tena Green started writing at age 11. In 2000, she took a journalist position for a local newspaper, *The Bellevue Gazette*, where she gained a priceless education from her editor and coworkers. While working for *The Gazette*, she wrote more than 300 articles and started doing freelance work.

Less than two years after starting as a journalist, she published her first novel, *The Catalyst* (2003), and has since written *A Woman's Touch* (2006); *X-30* (2007), a collaboration with friend and horror writer Richard Dean; and *Your First Year as a Principal: Everything You Need to Know That They Don't Teach You in School* (Atlantic Publishing 2009).

Prior to her writing career, Green raised four children and worked in the local schools as a volunteer, substitute secretary, intervention specialist, and teacher's aide. It was there that she realized her passion for children and their education.

Green is still writing novels, giving presentations for students on how to use reading and writing as an outlet, and writing books to help educators become effective and successful.

Index